HERE COME THE CLOWNS

By PHILIP BARRY

WAR IN HEAVEN

HERE COME THE CLOWNS

Here Come The Clowns

A PLAY IN
THREE ACTS

By PHILIP BARRY

COWARD-MCCANN, INC.

NEW YORK

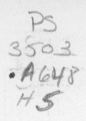

22833

To Adèle and Robert Abercrombie Lovett

Here Come the Clowns *was first presented by Eddie Dowling at the Booth Theater in New York City on December 5, 1938. It was directed by Robert Milton and the setting was designed by John Koenig.*

CHARACTERS

DAN CLANCY
NORA CLANCY
CONNIE RYAN
FREDDIE BALLANTINE
VAL GURNEY
JOHN DICKINSON
JIM MARBLE
GERT MARBLE
LEW COOPER
FAY FARREL
MAJOR ARMSTRONG
MAX PABST
MA SPEEDY
WALTER

ACTION AND SCENE

The play takes place in an American city on a Saturday night in late March, several years ago. The Action is continuous, beginning at about eleven o'clock in the Back Room of MA SPEEDY's *Café des Artistes, where it concludes two hours later. In the intervals between Acts no time is presumed to have elapsed.*

HERE COME THE CLOWNS

ACT I

ACT I

MA SPEEDY'S CAFÉ DES ARTISTES *is a long, narrow building extending from the corner of Front Street and Vine halfway down the block to the stage-alley of James Concannon's Globe Theater, of which it is a structurally integral part.*

The Back Room is MA SPEEDY'S *special and secret pride. There is a miniature stage, set into the back wall, flanked on either side by a small booth, on the same level. Red curtains, which pull from the side, now partially cover the stage. The booths can be used as dressing rooms when occasion demands, also by pulling curtains across them. The artists are given to trying out new acts here in the presence of their critical fellows and sometimes, when the spirit moves, spontaneous entertainments take place. From the booth at left a small, steep staircase mounts to a narrow balcony which stretches the length of that side of the room and leads into the dance hall which*

occupies the upstairs front of the build-
ing. In addition to the tables in the
booths, there are two other tables set on
ground level in each corner of the room,
and one in the center, facing the stage.

In the left wall there are two doors, the
large one giving access to the restaurant,
the smaller swinging one leading directly
to pantry and kitchen. Opposite them is
the private entrance from the alley, avail-
able only to the sacred and special few.
It is after the show on a Saturday night
in late March and the little lamps on the
tables are lighted and the gas log on the
alley-side aglow, making the room quite
cozy and inviting. In the booth at the
right sits MAJOR ARMSTRONG, *a copy of*
the then current "Billboard" propped up
before his face. This, and the long, check-
ered tablecloth almost completely hide
him from view. Certainly no one not
knowing him could be aware of the
cushion upon which he sits. JOHN DICK-
INSON, *also alone, occupies the opposite*
booth. A siphon and glass stand upon the

table before him and his head is down upon his folded arms.

The door from the alley has been cautiously opened not more than six inches. WALTER, *the waiter, stands there looking out, one hand securely grasping the door knob, the other flat on his flank, holding his apron down against the wind which blows up the alley on March nights such as this one. He speaks quietly to the two dim figures who stand in the half-light beyond the door.*

WALTER:

I'm sorry, ladies. You'll have to go to the front entrance. This is private.

A woman's voice, husky, pleasing, replies from outside the door.

CONNIE:

I know—but it was Mr. Gurney who sent us. He said just to mention his name.

WALTER:

I'm sorry, ladies, but Mr. Gurney would have to be with you.

Another woman's voice, frail, lighter, is heard.

NORA:

You know me—I've been here lots of times.

WALTER:

All the same, he'd have to be with you.

CONNIE:

He'll be along in a minute. He and Mr. Ballantine are just finishing counting up.

WALTER:

I'm sorry, but it's the rules. You'll have to wait for him in the front.

NORA:

Come along, Connie. I'm all right.

CONNIE:

Like fun you are. You need something and you need it quick.

Then again to the waiter.

Look, whatever your name is, it's raining. Please, will you?

WALTER:

You'll have to go around to the front. Just back down the alley and around. This room is strictly reserved for the artists from the Globe.

CONNIE:

But I tell you it was Val Gurney himself, who—

WALTER:

No one can come in without their private key or else accompanied.

14

NORA:

Come along, Connie.

CONNIE:

But she's sick, I tell you! She's had a shock. She's all in. She needs something. She needs something right away.

WALTER:

You must of made a mistake. This is no Speak. We don't serve a thing here. This is Ma Speedy's Café des Artistes, and strictly within the—

CONNIE:

Listen! Tell Ma Speedy for me that Connie Ryan, head usher at the Globe, is here with her sister who's had a shock!

WALTER:

I'm sorry, ladies. The proprietor is in the front. You'll have to ask there.—And *strictly* within the law.

> *He closes the door and waits a moment, his hand still on the knob, until he is sure they have gone. Then he moves to the booth nearest him and inquires cheerfully:*

What'll it be, Major Armstrong?

> *The voice that replies from behind "The Billboard" has its own peculiar quality:*

THE MAJOR:

A bottle of the Canadian ale, if you please.

WALTER:

The Molson's?

THE MAJOR:

The Molson's.

> WALTER *scratches upon his pad and moves toward the kitchen door. He is about to pass the second booth when the figure within it stirs and speaks.*

DICKINSON:

Wait.

> WALTER *stops and turns.* DICKINSON *slowly raises his head and drops both hands upon the table from the elbows. Then he lifts his face, smiling slightly, all like a machine capable of but one motion at a time. There are forty years in the face, every one of them, every day, every minute.*

What's the prodigious rush?

WALTER:

No rush, Mr. Dickinson, no rush at all.

DICKINSON:

Another double rye.

> WALTER *hesitates an instant.*

WALTER:

Are you sure?

DICKINSON:

Certainly I'm sure.

16

THE MAJOR:

—Also a small sandwich. Any kind.

> *He lowers the paper from before his face and the great head with its thin crest of white hair is for the first time visible.*

WALTER:

You know Ma don't want us serving food in here, Major.

> *So far as he can,* THE MAJOR *draws himself erect upon his bench. The patient eyes grow larger under their shaggy brushes. The fine, bony beak of a nose widens slightly with the intake of breath.*

THE MAJOR:

And you know I can't go in there and be stared at. Tell Ma who it's for.

WALTER:

If you say so, Major.

THE MAJOR:

Any kind but cheese.

WALTER:

I'll see what they have on hand.

DICKINSON:

And don't be so damned officious.

WALTER:

Ma expects us to exercise discretion, in the cases of—

DICKINSON:

Exercise it outside.

> WALTER *lowers his head, crosses and pivots through the swinging door. For a moment the two men sit staring out in front of them from their opposite cubicles, without speech. Finally, without turning his head,* THE MAJOR *addresses* DICKINSON.

THE MAJOR:

That must have been Clancy's wife at the alley door.

DICKINSON:

So I gathered.

THE MAJOR:

Then she must have been in the theater when it happened.

DICKINSON:

Ask me the three worst weeks in show-business—

THE MAJOR:

Three—let me see. Are there three?

DICKINSON:

Yes: the week before Christmas, Holy Week, and Naomi and her Violin.

THE MAJOR:

Very good. Very good indeed.

DICKINSON:

—So they combine two of them and wonder what

happens to business. They run in a number like Naomi and then tell me I don't know how to handle the publicity. Will you tell me how to get space for a female frog with a fiddle?

THE MAJOR:

Will you tell me what we can do about Clancy?

DICKINSON:

I wonder what it was that hit that crazy stagehand?

THE MAJOR:

Clancy's not crazy, John.

DICKINSON:

He gave a good imitation of it, stopping the show that way.

THE MAJOR:

It was the last number—and it was only Cooper and Farrel.

DICKINSON:

A swell world. A swell job all around.

THE MAJOR:

Poor Clancy.

DICKINSON:

—But the nerve of the guy, disappearing for a year, nobody knows where the hell to or at, then coming back out of the blue and right on stage in the middle of a turn and asking for someone!—Who, for God's sake?

THE MAJOR:

His wife, maybe.

DICKINSON:

No—he said "Sir."—*I* thought maybe Gurney.

THE MAJOR:

He could have gone straight to the box-office.

DICKINSON:

The house-manager?

THE MAJOR:

He saw Ballantine coming through from the front
and never blinked, even.

DICKINSON:

Damned if I know, then.

THE MAJOR:

All those misfortunes, one after the other: I guess
things just got to happening too fast for him.

DICKINSON:

He was a good mascot for the Globe, but he was a
bum one for himself, all right.

THE MAJOR:

He was always very religious: I hope it helps him.

DICKINSON:

The poor dope—the poor, bewildered dope. I was
there backstage a year ago when the baby-spot
came loose and caught him in the eye. It wasn't a
week since his kid died. And then, as if that wasn't

20

enough, that prize of a wife of his—well, as I say, it's a fine, pretty world.

THE MAJOR:

I'll never forget his white face tonight, staring out over those footlights.

DICKINSON:

What I'll never forget is what that whoozis—that swine of an illusionist—what he did afterwards.

THE MAJOR:

"Max" something—Max Pabst.

DICKINSON:

Pabst—that's it. He looked familiar somehow.

THE MAJOR:

I was so surprised when he appeared that way.

DICKINSON:

I could have killed him. I could have blown him right out of his upper box.

> *He half-rises, leans forward upon his table, assumes a bland expression and mimics the voice of a man speaking with a Middle European accent:*

"I wonder—I wonder could it be me—simple Max Pabst—for whom that poor, unfortunate stagehand was just now looking?"

> *And sinks back into his chair again.*

God! Anything for a cheap effect these days.

THE MAJOR:

It seems so, doesn't it?

> *The door from the restaurant opens and a short, stout, pink-and-white man comes in, carrying two vases of white carnations. He wears a dinner-coat, which drapes gracefully over his curves. He has very small feet and rotates upon them a trifle as he walks. His face is genial and kindly under its crown of wavy, unconvincingly reddish hair, and for all the fact that his features are now somewhat blurred by fat, one can see that he has once been handsome in his way. This is* MA SPEEDY *and he is in an expansive mood. He cries out in his musical voice:*

SPEEDY:

Good evening, John! Good evening, Major!

THE MAJOR:

Good evening, Ma.

DICKINSON:

Hello, Ma.

> WALTER *comes in with the drinks.* SPEEDY *places the carnations on the tables and stands off to view the effect.*

SPEEDY:

Everything all right?

22

DICKINSON:

Oh, just hunky-dory.

> WALTER *sets a glass, a bottle and a small sandwich before* THE MAJOR.

SPEEDY:

I wanted to see who was here. A couple of ladies just came in the front, and—do you remember our old friend Clancy, the stagehand?

DICKINSON:

We certainly do.

SPEEDY:

Well, it seems that one of them's his wife. Women and their nerves! I gather he's turned up again—I mean Clancy.

DICKINSON:

He certainly has.

SPEEDY:

The dance team, Cooper and Farrel—they just told me as they were going upstairs. I've never heard the like. Who do you suppose it is that he's after? Why wouldn't he at least say the name? You don't suppose he'll come wandering in here, do you?

DICKINSON:

I doubt it.

SPEEDY:

His wife needs a little refreshment, her sister says.

Shock.—And I wondered if vou'd mind them coming in here for a moment?

DICKINSON:

Not me. I'll move in with The Major.

> *He moves from his booth to* THE MAJOR'S.

SPEEDY:

I know they won't be long.

DICKINSON:

For all me, they can both get stewed to the eyes.

THE MAJOR:

Give us the cribbage set, Walter.

WALTER:

Cribbage.

DICKINSON:

A dollar says I'm going to beat the little pants off you.

THE MAJOR:

We'll see about that.

> WALTER *returns with the game.*

DICKINSON:

Privacy, Walter.

> WALTER *draws a red curtain partially around the booth, making* THE MAJOR *and* DICKINSON *invisible from the table near the restaurant door, through which* SPEEDY *now calls:*

This way, ladies! Right in here, please!

He glances about him.

—Cozy. Where will one find a cozier nook?

> NORA CLANCY *and* CONNIE RYAN *come in from the restaurant.* NORA *is slight and frail, somewhere in her pretty, middle twenties.* CONNIE *is two years older, without* NORA'S *cheap refinement of feature, but curiously vital and attractive. Her half-open coat reveals the blue uniform of a Globe usher. Her low, husky voice is full of strength and self-confidence.*

CONNIE:

Thanks, Mr. Speedy.

NORA:

Yes—thanks, I'm sure.

> SPEEDY *draws out chairs for them, flutters over them.*

SPEEDY:

Just sit yourselves doon and order what you like, only no food, please. Food in the front, sandwiches to write home about, a grilled chicken that would break your heart.

> NORA *and* CONNIE *seat themselves.* SPEEDY *claps his hands together.*

Walter!—Ask the ladies what they will have, Walter.

25

WALTER:

Yes, ladies?

CONNIE:

A beer for me and a double brandy for her.

WALTER:

With seltzer?

CONNIE:

With plain water.

SPEEDY:

Perfect. A perfect prescription for the nerves.—The really good brandy, Walter.

> *He looks knowingly at* WALTER, *who marks on his pad, tucks his pencil behind his ear and goes out into the pantry.*

We'll soon get the roses back into those pretty cheeks again!

NORA:

Thanks. I guess I could use a couple.

SPEEDY:

If anyone who comes in speaks to you, please don't mind. We're all just one big family here.

CONNIE:

We won't mind. Come one, come all.

SPEEDY:

It's really like a little club, you know—Ma Speedy's little nook for members of the N.V.A.—Artistes for Artistes, you know!

26

He purses his little mouth into an O and goes out again into the restaurant, whistling happily. CONNIE *scrutinizes* NORA *intently.*

CONNIE:

Stop shaking.

NORA:

I'm not shaking.

CONNIE:

You are and you're a fool, Nora.

NORA:

I—I can't help it.

CONNIE:

Clancy couldn't have seen you way up there in the balcony. He couldn't possibly have.

NORA:

It wasn't that.

CONNIE:

Then what was it?

NORA:

His voice. He—he acted so crazy.

CONNIE:

You think it's Val that he's after, don't you?

NORA:

I'm scared, Connie. I'm so scared.

27

CONNIE:

You know he's gentle as a baby. You know he wouldn't lift a finger to you.

NORA:

But Val—if he goes after Val—

CONNIE:

He doesn't even know it was for Val you walked out on him! He doesn't know it was for anyone, the poor innocent.

NORA:

He might of found out some way.

CONNIE:

How could he have? He left town two days after. And that was months ago.

NORA:

Someone might of wised him up—some busybody.

CONNIE:

Go on—it's nothing but your own guilty conscience.

NORA:

It was only while I was with him I had a guilty conscience.

CONNIE:

After a moment.

There are times I just don't get you at all.

NORA:

We're different, that's all. We always have been.

CONNIE:

I'll say we have.—But don't kid yourself that if Clancy's gone off his head it wasn't you who did it, because it was.

NORA:

It was not! It was not!

CONNIE:

All right, all right—calm yourself!—Anyway, I don't believe for a minute that he has.

NORA:

He was always half nuts—half the time he didn't make sense at all.

CONNIE:

You mean the kind of sense *you* could understand. You never had his imagination.

NORA:

Oh my God—"imagination"!

CONNIE:

You heard me.

NORA:

I know I did. And I know how you've always stuck up for him, regardless.

CONNIE:

Why shouldn't I have?—If ever a guy got a dirty deal from life *and* his wife—

29

NORA:

—Why? Lots of people have accidents and lose their jobs and have a kid die on them and—

CONNIE:

—*And* his wife, I said.

NORA:

Maybe you should of married him instead.

CONNIE:

Wha-at?

> *She laughs shortly.*

Me marry Clancy? That's a good one. I should've sailed right up to him, I suppose. I should've said, "Mr. Clancy, I know you've got an eye for a pretty face but I'm the girl for you, Mr. Clancy. Plain Connie Ryan, good and dependable."—Yes: I wouldn't've married him if he'd offered himself on a silver platter. Not if he'd come to me on his knees, I wouldn't've. Me married to Clancy! That really *is* to laugh.

NORA:

Maybe yes, maybe no. At least you could of plowed through all those foolish books with him and talked big talk till two in the morning on one glass of beer about God knows what. And of course *you'd* never of wanted to go to dances and things.

CONNIE:

Listen: I like dances just as much as you do! Clancy likes them too—if he goes with someone who sticks to him and doesn't roll her eyes around like a couple of hoops.

NORA:

Tell me one thing: how'd you like to be married to someone who made you feel mean all the time?

CONNIE:

Nobody could me.

NORA:

—When all you wanted was a little fun every other year or so.

CONNIE:

Show me somebody funnier than Dan Clancy when he wanted to be.

NORA:

I guess he just didn't want to be, with me: I guess that was it.

CONNIE:

I never had to wait around for the laughs with him.

NORA:

It's just what I'm telling you: *you're* the one who should of—

CONNIE:

Here's your drink.

> WALTER *swings in from the pantry and up to them with their orders.* CONNIE *fingers her purse.*

How much, Old Willie the Watch-dog?

WALTER:

Sixty and twenty-five: eighty-five.

CONNIE:

He can count.

NORA:

Val will settle for them when he comes.

CONNIE:

> *To* WALTER.

Mr. Gurney is doing the honors. Is that all right?

WALTER:

Sure thing. Why not?

> *He moves to the other table and wipes it off, around the vase of white carnations that stands upon it.* NORA *takes a swallow of her drink.*

NORA:

It's strong.

CONNIE:

You surprise me.

NORA:

—If only I could get him to hate me. If I could just simply get him to hate me.

32

CONNIE:

There's none of it in him—not for anyone.

> NORA *finishes her glass, then sits staring down into it, turning it in her fingers.*

NORA:

I don't know why a fellow like Clancy—a stage-hand who never made more than forty-eight a week at the most—I don't know why *he* should be so important, anyway.

> CONNIE *looks at her over her beer.*

CONNIE:

I don't know either. I wonder why he is?

> WALTER *has glanced up with sudden interest at the mention of* CLANCY'S *name.*

WALTER:

Is Clancy back?

CONNIE:

He's back.

WALTER:

How is he?

CONNIE:

Fine. They call him Lucky Dan he gets so many of the breaks.

> *A key is turned in the alley-door and* VAL GURNEY *comes in—a jaunty, tricked-out, sharp-featured little man of thirty. He sails his natty hat onto a hook on the wall,*

33

> *adjusts his cuffs and makes directly for the table where* CONNIE *and* NORA *sit, and bends over* NORA, *who brightens at his approach.*

GURNEY:

Well, well. Well, well, well!—I see you're taking your tonic, Baby.

NORA:

Hello, Val.

CONNIE:

I thought you were so well known here.

GURNEY:

You seem to have got in all right.

CONNIE:

Just like a couple of pianos through a transom.

GURNEY:

Exclusive, is what Ma's is.

> *He seats himself with them, takes one of* NORA's *hands in his and calls across his shoulder to the waiter:*

Make mine a Scotch highball, Walter m'boy!

> WALTER *continues his polishing.*

WALTER:

One Scotch.

GURNEY:

> *To* NORA.

34

Now don't you worry, sweetheart. Nothing's going to happen to you.

NORA:

I'm all right now.

GURNEY:

There's no way Clancy could've got onto the fact that we've been friends, that I can see.

CONNIE:

"Friends!"

GURNEY:

Now sister! Don't put your oar in again. Fingers out of other people's pies, sister. Little girls get burned.

CONNIE:

You're disgusting. You're just plain disgusting.

GURNEY:

And don't try to insult me. I been insulted by experts.

Then, to NORA.

You get upset too easy, dearie. It couldn't've been me he was looking for. Not old Val—not me. He'd've come right to my little cage in the lobby. Wouldn't he? Wouldn't he of?

NORA:

I guess so—yes, I guess so.

CONNIE:

And suppose he had?

35

GURNEY:

Suppose not, sister, lest ye be supposed.

CONNIE:

> *To* NORA.

How you can stand him!

NORA:

If you don't like it, you know what you can do.

CONNIE:

You said it.

> *She pushes her glass away and rises from the table.*

GURNEY:

> *To* NORA.

—Clancy don't know a thing, not one thing. Take my word for it. Walter m'boy—another for the lady!

WALTER:

One Scotch, one brandy.

> CONNIE *has crossed to the alley-door.*

CONNIE:

I suppose it's all right to go *out* this way?

WALTER:

Absolutely, lady, absolutely.

CONNIE:

Funny, the difference between two sides of a door.

> WALTER *moves toward the pantry.* CONNIE *opens the door. Halfway through it, she*

36

stops and listens up the alley, then re-enters, closing the door behind her, and moves swiftly back to the table. GURNEY *is reassuring* NORA.

GURNEY:

Baby—Baby!

NORA:

I'm all right, Val—I'm all right. The only thing that worries me is—oh, to hell with it.

> GURNEY *glances up at* CONNIE.

GURNEY:

What's up? Who asked for an encore?

CONNIE:

Get out. Get in there—quick! Get into the front!

NORA:

Oh my God, Val.

> NORA *rises,* GURNEY *after her.*

GURNEY:

We'll take our drinks in the front, Walter.

WALTER:

> *Going out.*

—Isn't allowed.

CONNIE:

Go *on!*

NORA:

I got to have another drink.

37

GURNEY:

> *To* CONNIE.

Will you keep him here?

CONNIE:

I don't guarantee anything.

NORA:

—I just simply got to.

> GURNEY *pilots* NORA *toward the restaurant door.*

GURNEY:

Listen, Honey, don't worry: there's something on the old hip. And we'll just sit ourselves right down and get outside of a nice welsh rabbit, or what would the lady like?

NORA:

No, no—I don't want anything to eat! All I want is—you keep him here, Connie—you hear me?

GURNEY:

—Now look, Honey: nobody's going to bust up Val Gurney's Saturday night snack with his own girl, believe you me—Clancy or nobody else. Who does he think he is, anyhow?

> *They go out into the restaurant.* CONNIE *reseats herself at the table with her back to the alley-door and pulls her glass toward her. Again a key turns in the lock and a boyish, discontented-looking young*

woman, GERT MARBLE, *enters, followed by*
JIM MARBLE, *a lanky individual of about
forty, and* DAN CLANCY. CLANCY *is prob-
ably somewhere in his middle thirties, but
with such lines of fatigue in his face, such
anxiety in his fearsome eyes as to make
any conjecture as to his actual age ir-
relevant and beside the point. One of*
MARBLE'S *arms is about his shoulders as
they enter, and in the crook of the other
he carries a bulky object in a large canvas
bag, like a duffle-bag.* MARBLE *is talking
very fast.*

MARBLE:

—And Frank's got the makings of a great dramatic
artist, see? And he's a personal friend of mine, but
what he don't know about business would fill a
book, see? And they're trying to sign him for a
series of twenty short subjects, so I go to the
Grossett office with him, see?

> MARBLE *puts the bag on the piano bench.*
> GERT *lights a cigarette and looks about
> her, distastefully.* MARBLE *continues to
> talk without pause.* CLANCY *sits staring
> out in front of him, barely listening.*

—And Jack Grossett himself, he starts to roll it
out.—And—

GERT:

This dump. Why do we do it?

MARBLE:

—And I say, "Talking pictures my eye. Who wants to hear shadows talk?" And he pounds the table and shouts, "They want sound. The public's crying for sound!" "Wrong," I say. "They don't know what they want till we give 'em it." "Just what I say," he says. "And we're going to give 'em sound."

> GERT *rises from the table. He turns to her.*

—Where you going, Gert?

GERT:

Give me some chips.

MARBLE:

What for?

GERT:

Food. I'm empty as a drum.

> MARBLE *takes two bills from a roll and gives them to her.*

MARBLE:

Don't be long.

GERT:

You bet.

> *She passes* CLANCY, *prods him affectionately.*

You're all right, Clancy.

40

MARBLE:

> *To* CLANCY.

—Where was I?

CLANCY:

What?

MARBLE:

I say, where was I?

CLANCY:

You were talking.

> GERT *goes out into restaurant.* MARBLE
> *settles back again.*

MARBLE:

I remember!—"We are not interested in your opin-
ions, Mr. Marble," he says. "But in the case of your
friend Frank here—" "So long as I'm taking care
of him," I say, "he's going to stay in vaudeville."
"Then he'd better get a new nurse," he says, "because vaudeville is not long for this world."—
Can you beat it?

CLANCY:

Can you beat it?

> *He shifts his position slightly and looks
> around him. His eyes fix upon* CONNIE'S
> *back at the table opposite him.* MARBLE
> *undoes the strings of the black bag and
> draws* THE DUMMY *out of it; he folds the*

41

bag into a cushion for THE DUMMY *and places it on the piano bench.*

MARBLE:

—There you are, Frank, my friend. Now mind you behave yourself.

THE DUMMY'S *grotesque mouth flaps open and shut.*

THE DUMMY:

God, how you love to hear yourself talk!

MARBLE *pushes him in the face.*

MARBLE:

Insect!

THE DUMMY *collapses face down upon the piano bench.* CLANCY *pronounces the name slowly, directly at* CONNIE'S *back.*

CLANCY:

Connie Ryan.

CONNIE *raises her head, without turning it.*

CONNIE:

Hello, Dan Clancy.

Then she turns and eyes him evenly.

You don't seem too glad to see me.

CLANCY'S *accent has not breadth enough for a brogue. It is only through a faintly musical intonation and an occasional odd locution that his Irish reveals itself.*

42

CLANCY:

I'm glad to see you.

CONNIE:

You look thin.

CLANCY:

You ought to see me sideways. How's Nora?

CONNIE:

She's all right.

CLANCY:

What's she living by? Is she working again?

CONNIE:

She is.

CLANCY:

There wasn t much she could do.

CONNIE:

How have you been?

CLANCY:

—She's flighty, you know. Nora's flighty.

CONNIE:

You're telling me—who brought her up from a baby?

THE DUMMY makes a snoring sound.

MARBLE:

—Disagreeable little mutt. When will you learn manners?

THE DUMMY:

Shut up and let me sleep.

43

CONNIE:

> *To* CLANCY.

—Tell me, how's it been going with yourself? I got to wondering about you once or twice, when I had a spare minute or two.

CLANCY:

I've been all over the place.

CONNIE:

So I heard tell, from the stage of the Globe to-night.

CLANCY:

That was a bad thing I did.

CONNIE:

Only for Cooper and Farrel—and they're young.

CLANCY:

All the same, it was bad and ill-mannered, interrupting the show that way. But I was almost out of my senses, Connie.

CONNIE:

And where are you now, would you say?

CLANCY:

The sight of you brings me back into 'em. You're the real foul-weather friend, Connie.

CONNIE:

You'll turn my head with your compliments.

CLANCY:

I'm a queer duck, and there's no denying it.

44

HERE COME THE CLOWNS

CONNIE:

Who is it you're after, Dan? Who've you been looking for?

> CLANCY *looks away.*

—I only thought I might maybe give you a steer.

CLANCY:

No, there's no one can do that.

CONNIE:

You certainly got all the bum breaks there were.

CLANCY:

You have to take what comes.

CONNIE:

—What they call "resignation."

CLANCY:

They do, and they call it well.

CONNIE:

If I were you, I'd get good and sore, believe me I would.

> *Suddenly* CLANCY *flares up.*

CLANCY:

Why should I? God damn it, it's the will of God!

> WALTER *comes swinging in from the pantry.* CLANCY *glances at him.*

Hello, Walter.

WALTER:

I heard you were back. I'm that glad to see you.

45

CLANCY:

It's good to be back.

WALTER:

What'll it be?

MARBLE:

Whisky for Clancy, whisky for me.

CLANCY:

Thanks, Jim, I don't want it.

MARBLE:

How do you know till you've tried?—Who's in the booth there, Walter? Anyone thirsty?

WALTER:

It's Mr. Dickinson and The Major.

> MARBLE *sets his mouth and the next instant from the inside of the booth, the yapping of a small dog is heard. The curtain is pulled roughly aside and* DICKINSON *is seen peering under the table.* MARBLE *laughs.*

MARBLE:

Look out—he bites!

> DICKINSON *looks out at him.*

DICKINSON:

Why, you low-life clown. You dirty low-life clown.

> *He comes down from the booth.*

—And who's this guy with you, with a face like the Coast of Kerry?

CLANCY:

Hello, John.

> *He takes* DICKINSON's *hand.*

How are you?

DICKINSON:

Drunk—and mean to get drunker. How's it with you?

CLANCY:

I'm fine. Why shouldn't I be?

DICKINSON:

Well, don't get tough about it. Who's the mystery-man you're trailing around theaters and such?

CLANCY:

If I told you, you still wouldn't know.

> THE MAJOR *calls from his booth.*

THE MAJOR:

Welcome home to you, Clancy!

CLANCY:

Thank you, Major. Welcome to yourself.

DICKINSON:

Drinks all around. This is a celebration.

THE MAJOR:

Ale for me, if you don't mind.

MARBLE:

Two. Gert likes ale.

47

CONNIE:

Three—one for me. That is, if I'm included.

> WALTER *goes out into the pantry.*

WALTER:

—Got 'em.

CLANCY:

You are all of you acquainted with Connie Ryan, my wife's sister?

MARBLE:

The fair Connie? I know her well.

> *Again he bends over* THE DUMMY.

And surely you remember my unpleasant little friend, Frank Frenzy?—Manners, Insect!

> THE DUMMY *sits bolt upright, grinning.*

THE DUMMY:

Hello, Connie! How's tricks?

CONNIE:

Hello, Frank! Fine!—How's with you?

THE DUMMY:

Couldn't be better.

> *He winks broadly.*

—So long as I get my liquor.

> *Again* MARBLE *pushes him in the face but this time he remains upright.*

CLANCY:

—And John Dickinson.

48

DICKINSON:

How are you, Connie?

CONNIE:

How-de-do, Mr. Dickinson.

DICKINSON:

Wearing the usher's uniform to bed these nights, are you?

CONNIE:

I—I came out in a sort of a hurry.

> CLANCY *gestures toward the booth.*

CLANCY:

—Major Armstrong, Miss Connie Ryan.

CONNIE:

Very pleased to meet you, I'm sure, Major.

> THE MAJOR *lets himself down from his cushion upon the bench, is lost to view for a moment as he comes under the table, and then emerges again from behind the tablecloth, the cushion under his arm. His tiny form—for now it is seen that* THE MAJOR *is a dwarf—negotiates the two steps to the floor-level, and stumps with dignity up to* CONNIE *and offers her a hand.*

THE MAJOR:

The pleasure is mine, Miss Ryan.

CONNIE:

I and the rest of the girls've enjoyed your act so much this week.

THE MAJOR:

I am sincerely glad.

MARBLE:

—Always a favorite with the ladies, eh, Major? Tom Thumb the Second.

THE MAJOR:

Do you know, they had General Tom Thumb in wax in Madame Tussaud's Museum in London for many years?

MARBLE:

You don't say!

CLANCY:

Did they, now!

THE MAJOR:

He stood there among other world notables, such as Napoleon and Nelson, and was the object of much interested comment.

> DICKINSON *takes the cushion from him and puts it upon a chair.*

DICKINSON:

Let's all sit.

> *He lifts* THE MAJOR *from the floor and places him upon the cushion.*

50

For God's sake, let us sit upon our bums and tell sad stories of the death of kings.

> *All, with the exception of* CLANCY, *seat themselves, all friends together, a new liveliness in their talk.*

THE MAJOR:

Don't misquote The Bard, John. That's not allowed even to scholars like you.

DICKINSON:

Scholars and scholarliness be damned together. Where are the drinks?

MARBLE:

You drink too much, see?

DICKINSON:

Or not enough—I was never sure. Clancy, I see in your eye that at last you agree with me it's one louse of a world.

CLANCY:

It can bite, can't it, John?

THE MAJOR:

—"The Best of All Possible Worlds," a book I know says.

DICKINSON:

For what? For whom?

MARBLE:

I guess we all of us have our troubles.

CLANCY:

That's right—and must be resigned to 'em.

DICKINSON:

A beautiful virtue, resignation.

CLANCY:

That's right.

DICKINSON:

Horse feathers.

THE MAJOR:

—Of course, the main thing is how we take them. That's where philosophy comes in.

DICKINSON:

Where philosophy comes in, is where I go out.

CLANCY:

If you were as hard as you think you are, John, they'd have split you up long since, and used you for coffin-wood.

DICKINSON:

I wish they had. It must be the rat-holes.

CONNIE:

This is a real gay party. This is certainly an evening out. When do the Australian Wood Choppers come on?

> *Again* MARBLE *sets his lips and from above them a falsetto voice is heard singing:*

52

THE VOICE:

"O dry those tears, O calm those fears. Life was not made for sorrow."

> THE DUMMY *twists his head around and looks up.* CONNIE *exclaims admiringly.*

CONNIE:

It's wonderful the way you do that, Mr. Marble.

MARBLE:

I'm a very wonderful fellow.

> CLANCY *glances toward the balcony.*

CLANCY:

What's that other sound I hear, like an orchestra?

> *He moves toward the restaurant.* CONNIE *follows him swiftly.*

CONNIE:

Don't go in there!

> *He stops. She explains:*

—They've had music upstairs since the first of the year. They dance there, eleven to one.

> CLANCY *speaks without interest.*

CLANCY:

Do they, now.

CONNIE:

> *After a moment.*

Dan—

CLANCY:

What?

CONNIE:

Do something for me?

CLANCY:

What?

CONNIE:

Will you promise to do it?

CLANCY:

I will if I can.

CONNIE:

You'll really promise?

CLANCY:

If I—

CONNIE:

No "ifs"!

CLANCY:

Then I will.

CONNIE:

Come up to the hall and dance a dance with me!

CLANCY:

Oh no, Connie—what are you talking about?

CONNIE:

You promised.

CLANCY:

But I've forgotten how. My feet wouldn't—

CONNIE:

You've not! It's not a thing, once known, you forget. It's like swimming or riding a bike—it stays with you.

> *She holds out both hands to him.*

Come on—one dance, like in the old days.

CLANCY:

God help me, I'll try.

> *She snatches a white carnation from the vase on the table, breaks the stem and fixes the flower in his lapel.*

CONNIE:

There! Now you look more like your old jaunty self!

> CLANCY *gazes down at the flower.*

CLANCY:

That's an odd thing. *He* always used to wear one, didn't he?

CONNIE:

Who did?

CLANCY:

A man I know.

> *Then his eyes look off into the far distance, across years, across waters.*

Carnations—my father used to raise them in the gardens of Roche's Hotel in Glengariff, where he worked. And my mother told me once the white one was the flower of God, God bless her. And we had a lemon tree, too. They grow there, you know. There's a warm current passes the coast. Figs, as well—even a palm now and then. My, how that lemon tree used to smell of a morning! It was glorious. It was like heaven.

> *He stops and passes his hand over his face.*

—And still I was always wanting to go to Connemara. I never got there, I don't know why. The good Lord willed it otherwise, I suppose.

THE MAJOR:

It was your father who wore the carnations?

CLANCY:

No. Never him. They were too dear, and must be kept for the table. But a man I know did—and you know him, too.

> *A moment's silence. Then* CONNIE *laughs lightly and slips her arm through his.*

CONNIE:

You and your lemon tree and carnations! Come along—you're day-dreaming!

> *She leads him to the stairway.*

Just remember one thing, dancing—they don't whirl about as they did.

> *They mount the stairs.*

CLANCY:

What is it they do, then?

56

CONNIE:

You'll see! It always came natural to you, Dan!
Once on the floor, you were like a man inspired.

CLANCY:

Me grandfather claimed he introduced the waltz
into Ireland.

> *They are moving along the balcony now.*

CONNIE:

> *Mocking him.*

—Me grandmother claimed she introduced Irish to
your grandfather.

CLANCY:

The language or the whisky?

CONNIE:

Both!—Will you promise to whirl me, Dan?

CLANCY:

That I will—like a top on a table!

> *There is a burst of music as they pass
> through the door and into the dance hall.*
> MARBLE *glances up, then takes a deep
> breath and settles down into his chair
> again. He replaces* THE DUMMY *in the bag
> and sets the bag upon the floor at his feet.*

MARBLE:

Well, I guess if he can dance—

DICKINSON:

—And if he can whistle very loud in the dark.

57

MARBLE:

He's like a man that's been hit over the head, isn't he?

DICKINSON:

Well, so he has—and I'd hate to count the times. *Unnoticed by them the door on the balcony again opens and a* FIGURE *appears there: a stoutish man of uncertain age, wearing a dark suit of foreign cut. His face is bland, and, in repose, curiously benevolent. What hair he has, is cropped short. He comes to the railing and stands there, looking out thoughtfully.* THE MAJOR *reflects:*

THE MAJOR:

It's true: *he* always did wear one.

DICKINSON:

Who wore what?

THE MAJOR:

I think I know now who it is Clancy wants to see—

DICKINSON:

Who?

THE MAJOR:

The Old Gentleman himself—the owner of the Globe, James Concannon.

58

MARBLE:

Go on—nobody ever sees Concannon any more.

DICKINSON:

—And very few in the past, did they?

THE MAJOR:

Clancy did now and then. So did I. I think it's to him he would naturally turn. In fact, I don't believe I've ever known one human being to reverence another as Clancy does James Concannon.

DICKINSON:

Concannon, my foot.

> *He rises and moves to the little stage.*

I'll bet the dust is deep on that private staircase of his, the old fake. Let's have a look. I even doubt if he's here at all any more.

> *He opens the stage curtains wide.* MARBLE *calls after him:*

MARBLE:

Well, if he isn't, where is he?

DICKINSON:

Ask Jack Grossett down in New York—he might tell you. Sure—just go right up to the door of Grossett Enterprises and say "How come we don't see Mr. Concannon, since your Mr. Jack went out to get him?"

> *He draws aside the spangled curtain which masks the brick wall at the back of the*

> *stage, and discloses a small door marked*
> "MR. CONCANNON. PRIVATE."

—Locked tight. I thought so. Where *is* the old fake? I'd really like to know. Who runs things now, anyway? Don't tell me Ballantine!

THE MAJOR:

Mr. Concannon is not a fake, John.—And I think Clancy came back tonight believing he'd be—

> THE FIGURE *on the balcony leans out and inquires in a low, precise voice with a Middle European accent.*

THE FIGURE:

—Or I wonder—I wonder could it be me, simple Max Pabst, for whom that poor, unfortunate fellow has been looking?

> DICKINSON *turns quickly and stares up at him.*

DICKINSON:

The great illusionist again, is it?—Listen: old bag of tricks, say that once more, and I'll—!

THE FIGURE:

—So sorry to disturb.

MARBLE:

Sit down, John.

> DICKINSON *reseats himself, muttering:*

DICKINSON:

What's he doing here tonight anyway? What's the

60

point of arriving in town two days ahead of time?
He doesn't go on until Monday, does he? Who ever
heard of an Act blowing in on a Saturday? Anyhow, I swear to God I've seen him some place.

> THE FIGURE *on the balcony comes quietly*
> *along it to the stairs.* SPEEDY *re-enters*
> *from the restaurant, calling back after*
> *him.*

SPEEDY:

This way, gentlemen! Right in here, Professor
Pabst!

> MARBLE *brings a loose deck of cards from*
> *his pocket and shows them to* THE MAJOR
> *who nods. They go to the table in the*
> *booth at right of the little stage and begin*
> *to deal out cold hands.* DICKINSON *hunches*
> *his chair nearer to his table and picks up*
> *his drink again.* FREDDIE BALLANTINE *en-*
> *ters, a dapper little middle-aged man in a*
> *dinner coat, carrying an umbrella.* SPEEDY
> *cries out in surprise:*

But where's the Professor?

> BALLANTINE *turns and looks back into the*
> *restaurant.* THE FIGURE *coming down the*
> *stairs speaks very softly:*

THE FIGURE:

Here I am.

SPEEDY:

Gracious! You're just everywhere at once, *you* are!

PABST:

A little tour: I like to see things for myself.
He looks around him.
Pleasant—how pleasant—a charming setting. Anything could happen here—no?

SPEEDY:

—This little nook is my pet, Professor!—*This* is the true Café des Artistes—isn't it, Freddie?

BALLANTINE:

Absolutely.

PABST:

—And a stage, also?

BALLANTINE:

We've absolutely even rehearsed here at times.
WALTER *re-enters.*

SPEEDY:

But it's chiefly for little informal entertainments —you know—just among ourselves, when the spirit moves us.
WALTER *places drinks before the card-players.*

DICKINSON:

Thanks. It's about time.

62

SPEEDY:

> *To* PABST.

Don't you think it's cozy?

PABST:

Very.—Full of what-you-call-it—*gemütlichkeit.*

SPEEDY:

Oh, I love that word! It's just the word for it!

PABST:

Take it—take it for your own.

SPEEDY:

"*Gemütlichkeit.*"

> *Ballantine draws out chairs at the other table.*

BALLANTINE:

His liquor's all right. I'll grant him that.

SPEEDY:

Bring a bottle of the "Perfection," Walter.

> *He explains.*

We're serving "Perfection" now. It's really quite good.

> *He calls to the other table.*

Hello, fellows!—Got every little thing you want?

MARBLE:

Sure thing.

THE MAJOR:

Yes, indeed.

63

DICKINSON:

And a couple we don't.

> WALTER *goes out.* SPEEDY *seats himself with* BALLANTINE *and* PABST.

BALLANTINE:

What a night! I never made such a long speech in my life.

PABST:

But an explanation to the audience was indicated, was it not?

BALLANTINE:

Just let Clancy try something like that again. Just once more.

SPEEDY:

Poor Cooper and Farrel. I never heard of such a thing happening.

> *He ponders a moment.*

Except once, I remember, at Keith's in Washington, a cat walked on stage right in the middle of my act. It was one of the worst ordeals I've ever gone through. I was in the middle of the Prayer from *La Tosca* and, you know, the House threatened to get quite out of hand.

PABST:

I have no doubt.

64

SPEEDY:

Well, sir, you know what I did? I held the top note as long as I could—

> *He arches the fingers of one hand upon his bosom and elevates the other hand like a chalice. He throws back his head and in a shrill falsetto sings a line from the aria.*

—I can't get up there any more. Then I let—quite unexpectedly, you know—I let out a long "meaow"

> *He demonstrates, and finds his lower register again.*

Well, sir, they loved it! They laughed with me, not at me. They were absolutely mine.

PABST:

An inspiration—a most happy inspiration.

SPEEDY:

Those were the days. Three years running, I was held over a second week at The Palace. I had a special curtain and drop of my own—a living mass of sequins. Harry Collins made my gowns. I traveled with six trunks and had thirty-two changes. All New York was mad about me. I had a cigar named after me.

PABST:

Those must, indeed, have been the days.

BALLANTINE:

You should have stuck it out a little longer, Ma.

SPEEDY:

I couldn't, Freddie. I simply couldn't.

> *To* PABST.

—I don't know about in Europe, but here, in some way, the War changed the audience's attitude toward my kind of art. Well, sir, I saw the handwriting on the wall, as they say—so I just bought this little nest and settled down in it. In a way it was a relief: I could eat all I wanted to at last and see all my old friends as they came through and just sit back and let my figure go—and don't you think it's cute?—My little set-up here, I mean.

PABST:

Gemütlich.

SPEEDY:

Ja—ganz gemütlich.

> WALTER *re-enters with drinks from the pantry, and* GERT *from the restaurant.*

That's right, Walter.—Good evening, Gert.

GERT:

Hello, Ma.

> *She proceeds to the table in the booth and seats herself with* MARBLE *and* THE MAJOR *as* WALTER *places drinks before* SPEEDY, BALLANTINE *and* PABST.

SPEEDY:

—The wife of the ventriloouist you saw tonight. She assists.

PABST:

He was very good.

MARBLE:

> *To* GERT.

Where've you been all this time?

GERT:

I got to talking.—You know the kid I got the fan note from yesterday?

MARBLE:

What about her?

GERT:

She was in the Front—and guess what.

MARBLE:

What?

GERT:

She's spending next week in Syracuse too—with friends.

> MARBLE *slams down his cards.*

MARBLE:

The hell she is!

GERT:

Why? What's the matter?

HERE COME THE CLOWNS

MARBLE:

I'll show you what's the matter. I'll show her, too!
See?

GERT:

Is he drunk?

THE MAJOR:

Would you like a hand?

GERT:

Sure. All aces, please.

> She glances contemptuously at MARBLE.
> He picks up his cards again, still watching
> her under his eyelids. She murmurs:

Try not to be more of a fool than God made you.

> The game proceeds. BALLANTINE turns to
> PABST, who has been listening attentively
> to the altercation at the other table.

BALLANTINE:

You haven't said how you liked the rest of the bill.

PABST:

On the whole, very much. Well selected and well
arranged. I was particularly interested in the performance of the Irishman who afforded me such a
what-you-call-it—good build-up—

BALLANTINE:

Clancy.—Yes—some performance! Absolutely!

> DICKINSON turns in his chair.

68

PABST:

I think he is a natural comic.

DICKINSON:

Horse feathers.

PABST:

I beg your pardon?

DICKINSON:

A comic, eh?—That's most discerning of you, I'm sure.

BALLANTINE:

Come on over.—I want you to meet the Professor.

> DICKINSON *makes his way to them a little too steadily.*

—Professor Max Pabst—Dickinson, our press man.

> PABST *rises and bows stiffly.*

DICKINSON:

How do you do, I'm sure.

BALLANTINE:

He'll absolutely want to ask you a few questions for the Monday press.—Sit down, John.

> DICKINSON *and* PABST *seat themselves.* DICKINSON's *manner is definitely antagonistic.*

DICKINSON:

I must have caught your Act somewhere.

PABST:

You have traveled much in Europe?

69

DICKINSON:

No. Not any.

PABST:

Then it is not possible.

DICKINSON:

But you look familiar.

PABST:

That is an impression I often give. It is part of my what-you-call—stock in trade.

DICKINSON:

—Got the usual advance stuff with you, I suppose.

PABST:

Unhappily no.

BALLANTINE:

He came on in such a hurry. When La Paloma took sick in Detroit—

DICKINSON:

—We were stuck for an Easter Week headliner, sure. But how'd we happen to get such a break as the Professor?

PABST:

I was in the Grossett Offices in New York when the telegram came about the sudden illness of the Thinking Horse.

DICKINSON:

—So you leaped right into La Paloma's shoes, eh?

70

PABST:

On an impulse, I offered myself as substitute.

DICKINSON:

There's something phoney about this. Maybe Jack Grossett did oust Concannon out, back there when he thought he'd run vaudeville, north and south, east and west—himself, single-handed. Maybe he's had you here all along. Maybe, in fact, you're the present Concannon.

PABST:

An amusing idea, but no.

DICKINSON:

You and Ballantine aren't in cahoots, of course?

BALLANTINE:

Cahoots! Me?

PABST:

"Cahoots"—what is that?

DICKINSON:

It's cahoots. Anyhow there's an idea around that it's Concannon our friend Clancy was looking for tonight.

PABST:

Really? How very interestin'. I met the old gentleman once or twice in years past. He was most impressive.—He seemed to me a very lonely man—but then who, of any importance, is not?

71

BALLANTINE *thrusts a piece of paper at* DICKINSON.

BALLANTINE:

Here's the change in the program copy. You'll absolutely have to check it.

DICKINSON *takes it and looks it over. At the next table,* MARBLE *leans to* GERT, *speaking lowly.*

MARBLE:

You'll have to head her off. See?

GERT:

Who?

MARBLE:

Your new Little Number.

GERT:

God, what a mug you can be.

MARBLE'S *hand falls on her arm.*

MARBLE:

You heard me. It's bad enough having to play a split-week like Syracuse, without any of that going on.

GERT:

I don't know what you mean.

MARBLE:

You heard me!

SPEEDY *glances at them.* PABST *has already been listening intently.* SPEEDY *calls gaily:*

72

SPEEDY:

Now, now! No domestic strife, please!

MARBLE:

Out! This is a private conversation.

> THE MAJOR *inquires mildly over his cards:*

THE MAJOR:

Are we playing?

GERT:

> *To* MARBLE.

Behave yourself, you!

> MARBLE *removes his hand and stares at his cards, swearing softly under his breath.*

MARBLE:

What a load I've taken on. God! Will it never end?

GERT:

If you can't take it, you know what to do.

THE MAJOR:

Please. I can't think.

SPEEDY:

> *To* PABST.

And they're really the most devoted couple, you know.

PABST:

Very interestin', very—

> DICKINSON *puts the paper in his pocket.*

73

DICKINSON:

This ought to be all right, *mutatis mutandis*. Just the usual crap.

PABST:

You seem a trifle—shall we say, unfriendly?

DICKINSON:

I guess the fact is I've never cared much for magicians.

PABST:

But I am not a magician.

DICKINSON:

Then what are you?

PABST:

An illusionist.

DICKINSON:

What's the difference?

PABST:

There is a great one. Magicians are interested primarily in deception. I am interested only in truth. —But truth is so often an illusion I must, you see, in truth call myself an illusionist.

DICKINSON:

—A new slant on the same old tricks: crap and double crap.

PABST:

Not "tricks," I beg of you. I am not interested in tricks. I have a modest gift for eliciting the truth,

74

that is all.—For instance, you carry a gun. Is that not the truth?

DICKINSON:

> *After a moment.*

Yes. Very clever. How did you know?

PABST:

That is not interestin'. What is interestin', is the purpose for which you carry it.

DICKINSON:

—And what might that be?

PABST:

Yourself.

> DICKINSON *stares at him.*

—But I wouldn't, if I were you. It would help nothing.

DICKINSON:

Thanks for the advice.

PABST:

—Merely the truth. Amusing to audiences because one sees and hears so little of it—particularly about oneself, you know.

> *He turns to* BALLANTINE.

Tell me more of your man Clancy. I find him most interestin' also. I should like to see more of him.

DICKINSON:

You won't have to wait long: he's upstairs now.

75

SPEEDY:

Here? You don't mean it!

DICKINSON:

Upstairs, I said. Dancing.

PABST:

So? I must have missed him.

BALLANTINE:

Dancing! Absolutely!

DICKINSON:

You know how they do—on volcanoes?

SPEEDY:

Oh dear—I don't like this at all!

PABST:

He is a natural comic. I hope I may be able to do something for him—something, perhaps, to help him forget his troubles.

DICKINSON:

I'm sure he'd appreciate that no end.

PABST:

Such a curious search of his—for whom—for what?

DICKINSON:

You tell us, Professor.

> PABST *gazes at him for a moment. Then speaks in a brisk, matter-of-fact voice to* SPEEDY:

76

PABST:

I hope my bag of effects will be safe in the coat-room?

SPEEDY:

Don't you worry. No one's ever lost even a hat at Ma Speedy's.

PABST:

And that was his wife in the Front, with her lover?

SPEEDY:

Well, they do say she and Gurney are—of course *he* doesn't *dream*—

> CLANCY's *voice is heard from the balcony above.*

CLANCY:

This way, Lew! Come along, Fay!

PABST:

Shh! *Jetzt kommt er. Er ist punkt.*

> *He looks up at the balcony from which a brief blare of music is heard as the door from the dance hall is opened, admitting* CONNIE *and* CLANCY, *who stand there, waiting for their companions.* PABST *smiles in anticipation. He speaks softly:*

Yes, we must see—we must certainly see what we can do for this unfortunate clown.

> CONNIE *and* CLANCY *still wait, and* PABST *watches.*

Curtain

HERE COME THE CLOWNS

ACT II

ACT II

The Same.

The positions are the same as at the end of Act One. The time is immediately after it. The action is continuous.

CONNIE *and* CLANCY *are joined on the balcony by the dance team,* LEW COOPER *and* FAY FARREL, *a slim, youthful and engaging pair, who enter from the dance-hall and precede them along the balcony toward the stairs.*

FAY:

Honest, I never had such a whirl in my life!
All are laughing and seem very merry as they come down the stairway.

CLANCY:

—And the night at the Beach, when we danced in the marathon—you remember, Lew? Fay, do you remember?

FAY:

My feet hurt yet, when I think of it.

81

CONNIE:

I've still got the doll we won.

CLANCY:

Have you, now!—It was a big doll.

CONNIE:

It still is. The fact is, it's grown three or four inches.

LEW:

Connie, I could fall for you!

> *And without warning he falls down the last half dozen steps and lies prone on the floor at the bottom.* MA SPEEDY *springs up with an exclamation, then sits down again as* FAY *walks calmly over* LEW.

SPEEDY:

—Now *that's* why I like this place!

> CLANCY *looks down admiringly.*

CLANCY:

I'd give my left arm to be able to do that, Lew.

CONNIE:

Only you couldn't without it.

> FAY *moves up to the empty table at the Left.*

SPEEDY:

They're song-and-dance: Cooper and Farrel.—And that's Clancy.

82

PABST:

I know.

> CONNIE *and* CLANCY *step over* LEW'S *still prostrate form.*

CONNIE:

Oh that music, that music!

CLANCY:

Wasn't it grand? It went right to my feet.

MARBLE:

> *To* THE MAJOR.

The boy's better.

THE MAJOR.

Much.

> LEW *picks himself up and follows the others to the table, calling to the waiter.*

LEW:

Beer all around, Walter.

WALTER:

Four beers—count 'em—four.

> *He goes out again into the pantry.*

FAY:

How long ago was it we all went to the Beach together?

CONNIE:

Three years Decoration Day.

CLANCY:

Where was Nora that night?

CONNIE:

She was laid up with a cold—don't you remember?

CLANCY:

That's right.

CONNIE:

I named the doll after you, Clancy.

CLANCY:

Did you, now.

FAY:

Fay Jack of the Jack Sisters, I was named after.

LEW:

I was named after nobody.

FAY:

You don't mind, though!

LEW:

The hell I don't.—How'd you like to be called something the top dame in an orphan asylum made up for you?

FAY:

I wouldn't mind.
> *She mocks him, singing:*
"No foolin', who do you love? Who are you thinking of, no foolin'?"
> *At the other table,* DICKINSON *lets his arms down wearily.*

84

DICKINSON:

If we had numbers for names, someone would try to make 7 stand out over 4.

BALLANTINE:

Absolutely!

DICKINSON:

7 grows a beard, and 4 goes to night-school.

PABST:

Quiet! Quiet, and listen! This is most interestin'.

LEW:

You'd more or less like to know who you are though, wouldn't you?

FAY:

"No foolin', who do you miss, when it's time to kiss, no foolin'?"
She stops singing, and replies:
I wouldn't care! Really I wouldn't.
She cocks her head gaily up at him.
Are names the reason you won't marry me?

LEW:

They might be.—And that ugly mug, of course.

FAY:

This guy has been crazy for me for five years, nearly. Ever since we teamed up and developed our act, he has. And still he won't marry me. He won't even sleep with me.

85

LEW:

Nary a wink, so lay off.

He leaves the table and moves to the piano bench.

CLANCY:

He's the deep one, Lew is. You need a long line with Lew.

LEW *begins to play* FAY's *song softly upon the piano.* CONNIE *has been shaping her napkin into a cone. She sets it up before her upon the table.*

CONNIE:

Night and day he stands up there on my dresser like this, that doll does. "Dan Clancy," I say to him, "you keep out of trouble. You're always getting into trouble."

CLANCY:

I must have been named after Daniel in the Lion's Den.

CONNIE:

"If you were troubled with lions," said the King, "you must have brought them yourself."

CLANCY:

If my little Angela had been a boy, I was going to name *her* after Michael the Archangel.

FAY:

Who? What circuit does he play?

CONNIE:

Listen to her!

CLANCY:

The Universal! Up the heavens and down again. He's captain of the selfsame troops that defended the throne of God against the assault and battery of the Old Nick, that time there was the trouble.

DICKINSON:

"And there was War in Heaven!"

CLANCY:

There was that all right—and what a war! My mother told me all about it, over and over. Three hundred years it went on. Of course, their time is not like ours.

CONNIE:

Three days, most likely—or else three minutes.

DICKINSON:

"Michael and his angels fought against the Dragon. And the great Dragon was cast out into the Earth."

    To PABST.

I thought you looked familiar.

PABST:

You are so amusing.

CLANCY:

Anyhow, Michael's the fine old bird, and without him God knows where we'd be now.

87

DICKINSON:

And where are we?

CONNIE:

And don't be so irreverent, calling him an "old bird."

CLANCY:

I'm not. I know The Captain well.—Once in the army—the time I got conked—I thought I saw him.
He salutes.
—Maybe I did.

CONNIE:

Oh, sure.

FAY:

I'll tell you what, Clancy: if Lew ever marries me and we have any kids I'll name the first one "Michael Daniel," after you both.

CLANCY:

You can leave out the "Daniel"—or call the next one it.
Abruptly LEW *stops his playing.*

LEW:

Oh, lay off this marrying-and-kids stuff! It's enough to drive a guy crazy!

FAY:

Why, Lew—

LEW:

—Just lay off it! Talk sense!

88

FAY:

He's been this way all week—some chip on his shoulder for everything and nothing.

LEW:

Well, it's been one hell of a week—playing to empty houses—and on the same bill with a flock of midgets. Midgets—God!

> CONNIE *glances in the direction of* THE MAJOR.

CONNIE:

Hush, Lew—

LEW:

I don't care. I hate 'em. I hate the sight of 'em.

> WALTER *re-enters.*

Hey, come on! Come on with those drinks, will you? I want a drink!

> PABST *leans confidentially toward* DICKINSON *and murmurs:*

PABST:

He does not know who he is, he will not marry— and he dislikes midgets.—Isn't it interestin'?

DICKINSON:

No.

> MAJOR ARMSTRONG *lays down his hand.*

THE MAJOR.

I think this is mine.

GERT:

> You think wrong. Look!
>> *She lays down hers.* MARBLE *examines both hands and pushes* GERT'S *back to her impatiently.*

MARBLE:

> Your mind's wandering.

GERT:

> But with three jacks and a pair of—

MARBLE:

> —And wandering where?
>> WALTER *comes up to them and puts a folded note on the table before* GERT.

WALTER:

> A young lady in the Front asked would I bring this note to you.
>> GERT *is about to pick up the note but* MARBLE'S *quick hand reaches it first.*

GERT:

> You give that here!
>> MARBLE *opens it and reads it, then crumples it up and flings it upon the floor.*

MARBLE:

> God! it's sickening. God, it makes me want to vomit.

90

GERT:

Get down on your knees and pick it up and give it to me.

MARBLE:

What am I to do with you? How can I keep you off it, you filthy, underhanded little—

> SPEEDY *rises and calls.*

SPEEDY:

Jim—Jim Marble!

MARBLE:

What do you want?

> SPEEDY *smiles and shakes his finger at him.*

SPEEDY:

—Please, Jim, for the sake of the rest of us.

> MARBLE *gestures him away.* GERT *rises, finds the note and reads it.* MARBLE *mutters.*

MARBLE:

How is a man supposed to stand it? Tell me, some-one—tell me, will you?

> GERT *tucks the note into her bosom, returns to the table and begins unconcernedly to deal out another hand.* PABST *smiles to himself and murmurs:*

PABST:

Perfection.

> SPEEDY *slides the bottle toward him, but that is not what he means. He repeats:*

Simple perfection.

BALLANTINE:

What?

PABST:

—As fine a collection of wretched, unhappy human beings as ever it has been my privilege to behold.

DICKINSON:

So what?

PABST:

Oh, nothing—nothing at all. The world in miniature—the variety-show *par excellence*—we cannot but regard it with pity. We must not be too amused.

> BALLANTINE *half rises.*

BALLANTINE:

Let's go.

PABST:

Oh no—no, I beg of you! I am learning so much.

BALLANTINE:

One more drink, then.

SPEEDY:

Oh yes—at least!

> *He claps his hands together.*

Walter!

WALTER *turns to him.*

Freshen us up, Walter.

BALLANTINE:

One—and one only.

> WALTER *nods and goes out into the pantry.* PABST *has turned and is gazing intently at the other table. Finally he calls very softly:*

PABST:

Mr. Clancy? Oh—Mr. Clancy!

CLANCY:

Me?

PABST:

You—yes.

> *He beckons him to them.*

Come—join us for a moment.

CLANCY:

Thank you—but it's—it's my friends I'm among here.

PABST:

A moment—only for a moment. Come—

> *Reluctantly* CLANCY *rises and moves to the table.*

DICKINSON:

He thinks you're wonderful, Clancy. He wants to marry you.

93

PABST:

> *To* BALLANTINE.

Introduce us, please.

BALLANTINE:

Dan Clancy—former chief stagehand—meet the great Professor — world-famous Illusionist — fresh from European triumphs—next week's headliner in place of La Paloma, who has the heaves in Detroit. —And maybe you'll tell me what you meant by coming on stage and ruining our show tonight?

CLANCY:

Good evening to you, Professor.—I'm sorry about it, Mr. Ballantine. It was impolite and unthinking of me.

BALLANTINE:

Haven't we absolutely done everything that could have been for you?

CLANCY:

Mr. Concannon has always been very kind.

BALLANTINE:

Mr. Concannon was away. It was me who slipped those extra bills in your envelope.

CLANCY:

You were very kind.—And is he returned, as yet?

BALLANTINE:

No—at least, I don't think so.

> SPEEDY *glances toward the stage.*

SPEEDY:

That stairway of his hasn't been used since I don't know when. I know, for I looked. I picked the lock.

DICKINSON:

There's a rumor around it's the Old Man himself you came back to see, Clancy.

> *At the next table* THE MAJOR *folds his cards into a book and listens. In fact, by now they are all listening.* CLANCY *shakes his head.*

CLANCY:

No, it was not.

> *He thinks a moment.*

Mr. Concannon is a great and a noble man and always was. I've never in my life known a better or finer, but—

> *And another moment. Then thoughtfully, to himself:*

—And to be sure, he might take that form as well as another, I suppose. But—

PABST:

"Form"?

DICKINSON:

Who might?

CLANCY:

I don't like to say. It's a personal matter between me and him.

95

MARBLE:

What *is* this?

> *There is a silence. At last* PABST *leans toward* CLANCY *and speaks very softly:*

PABST:

Mr. Clancy—

> CLANCY *turns to him.*

—Unhappy and luckless Mr. Clancy—is it possible, by some curious chance, that he for whom you have been searching is no less a personage than—

CLANCY:

Stop where you are!

PABST:

—Than God Himself?

> *Another silence. Then* CLANCY *raises his head proudly.*

CLANCY:

It is!—And what's there curious about it?

CONNIE:

Dan! What are you talking about?

SPEEDY:

Good gracious!

DICKINSON:

—A still hunt for the Almighty! It's marvelous.— Clancy, you certainly fly high.

> CLANCY *wheels on him and demands:*

96

CLANCY:

And why not? Isn't He everywhere? Is there a nook or a corner where He's not? What's there so strange in going out to find Him? Others have done it, and others will again!

> *Once more his head sinks and his wild eyes stare blankly at the floor. He goes on, half to himself:*

I have to find Him! 'Tis a necessary thing to me. I have some things to ask Him which nobody else can answer. I know it is His will that things happen as they do, but I've come to a place where I have to know the reason for certain of them.—And know I will!

PABST:

Of course, of course—

MARBLE:

It's the damnedest thing—

THE MAJOR:

Why, Jim?

BALLANTINE:

But in a Vaudeville House—on a Saturday night! Absolutely!

SPEEDY:

Yes—that takes the cake, it certainly takes the—

97

MARBLE:

Why, of all places, did you think He'd pick the Globe for a personal appearance?

CLANCY:

I don't know.—I was in Cleveland. I'd been many other places among the poor and the lowly, where they say it's easiest to—where they say He spends much of His time—but nor hide nor hair of Him. I was out walkin' by myself when all of a crack it came over me, like a cat jumped down on my back from a wall: "Tomorrow night at James Concannon's Globe—Holy Saturday night—hurry, me boy, hurry!"—So I came as quick as I could. I don't know how I got here. I don't even remember the—the train, it must have been. It wasn't till near curtain-time did I arrive. The sweat was pouring from me, for fear of missing Him—

His voice rises.

But I can't have! I can't! I know in my bones He was there!

Swiftly CONNIE *moves to his side.*

CONNIE:

Come along now, Dan. Come along with Connie.

CLANCY *pulls away from her.*

CLANCY:

Don't treat me as if I was bereft of my senses! I'm not!—I'm sane as the next one, maybe more so. I

98

could be a bit off on my reckoning, of course.—
Maybe it was tomorrow night—no, tomorrow's Sun-
day and the House will be locked fast, and dark.
—Or maybe it was somewhere not precisely *in* the
Globe, but roundabouts. Maybe it was even—even—
> *He glances about him.*

—No, Connie—the night's not over yet.

CONNIE:

Will you please to come along, please?

CLANCY:

And maybe miss Him entirely?—After all this time
render me search null and void?

> PABST *rises and touches his elbow and
> gently steers him into a chair at the table,
> then turns and calmly surveys the incredu-
> lous faces about him.*

PABST:

This seems not at all as strange to me as it appears
to seem to you. A man searches for the Truth and
calls it "God"—Why not? It has many names, and
as many faces.

CLANCY:

—It has one: and that's the name and the face of
God!

99

DICKINSON:

> *To* PABST.

Maybe you can scare Him up for the poor guy, Professor. Maybe *you* can evoke Him.

PABST:

The Truth, I can evoke.

DICKINSON:

Who says?

PABST:

You do not believe me.

DICKINSON:

No.

PABST:

You would like a demonstration, perhaps?

> *There is a silence. Then:*

DICKINSON:

Yes. Strut your stuff.

MARBLE:

—And be sure you make it good.

PABST:

Very well.—But you must promise not to interfere. —Agreed?

> DICKINSON *gestures assent.* PABST *moves swiftly to the little stage and mounts it.*

SPEEDY:

An entertainment! Oh, good! I did hope there'd be!

100

*He rises to view the stage. Suddenly he
cries out angrily:*

Those drapes! Who touched those drapes?

DICKINSON:

I did.

SPEEDY:

Well—you shouldn't have!

> PABST *tries the private door, finds it fast,
> then carefully draws the spangled curtains
> together again over it.*

PABST:

—And surely if He should choose to reveal Himself, Truth would prepare the way for Him,
would it not?

> *He arranges a chair and table at the cen-
> ter of the little stage.* BALLANTINE *rises
> and picks up his hat and umbrella.*

BALLANTINE:

I've had enough for one week. Goodnight, all.

> *He moves toward the alley-door.*

Me, I take Sundays off. I absolutely do my theater-
going on week-days.

> BALLANTINE *goes out.* PABST *comes for-
> ward upon the stage and inquires:*

PABST:

Shall we begin?

FAY:

Look, Lew—he's going to do his Act!
> *She moves to the piano bench and seats herself beside* LEW.

PABST:

Act?—I have no Act. It is you who have the Acts.
> *He descends the steps and turns to* MARBLE.

Mr. Marble—please—

SPEEDY:

But—but aren't *you* going to do *some*thing?
> PABST *smiles his slow, intolerable smile and levels his palms.*

PABST:

I? Oh no—*I* shall merely be master of ceremonies.
> *He turns again to* MARBLE.

You are a ventriloquist, I understand.

MARBLE:

That's the old rumor about me.

PABST:

And this is your wife with you?

MARBLE:

Yes, you might call her that.

GERT:

Don't turn my head, will you?

PABST:

—And you have your little man there in the black bag.

A muffled voice is heard from the bag:

THE DUMMY:

Let me out! Let me out!

PABST:

At once, little man.

To MARBLE.

Your wife assists you?

MARBLE:

In black tights: she has a fine figure, they say.

GERT:

—And don't fail to tell us everything.

PABST:

You will not need an assistant tonight. Take your place on the stage, please.

MARBLE:

Listen, Professor: I've played twelve performances this week and I'm weary, see? I'm throatsore and weary.

THE DUMMY:

From the bag.

Me too! Me too!

PABST:

Without accent.

This will refresh you both.

103

DICKINSON:

At times your English is better than at others.

PABST:

Danke. Thank you very much.—Well, Mr. Marble?

> MARBLE *rises, draws* THE DUMMY *from the bag and makes his way toward the stage.* SPEEDY *follows him, turns a switch at the side of the stage and lights a spotlight which casts a brilliant circle of light directly upon stage-center.* DICKINSON *drags himself to his feet and stands swaying, bracing himself against the table.*

DICKINSON:

Marble's too good for Number One on any bill. I'll do the opener: it's a recitation, very short and to the point. Listen, Clancy—this is for you—

> MARBLE *mounts the little stage and arranges himself there on the chair in the circle of light, a whisky-glass, a package of cigarettes and an ash-tray upon the table beside him, as* DICKINSON *proceeds:*

Once there was a little man like you in County Kerry—and he led a little life—and one day he began to pack a little bag. And *They* said, "Where are you off to? Where are you going?" And *he* said, "I'm packing my bag and I'm going to Connemara." And They said, "You mean, you're going to Connemara, God Willing." And he said, "I mean I'm going to Connemara."—So God changed him into a frog and put him in a frog-pond and kept him there for seven years.

CONNIE *laughs.*

CONNIE:

What kind of a God would do that to a little man?

DICKINSON:

Oh—Clancy's—and yours—and other people's generally. —And then God changed him back again—and what did the little man do? He began at once to pack his little bag.—And They said, "Where are off to? Where are you going?" And he said, "I'm going to Connemara." And They said, "You *mean,* you're going to Connemara, *God Willing.*" And he said, "I mean I'm going to Connemara, or back to the frog-pond!"

He gestures drunkenly toward CLANCY *and reseats himself.*

CLANCY:

I see what you mean.

DICKINSON:

—When you arrive there, send me a postcard.

CLANCY:

A postcard?

DICKINSON:

A postcard—with the answer.

PABST:

Apt—but we must have no more interruptions.

> *He turns to* MARBLE, *who now has* THE
> DUMMY *astride his knee.*

Shall we begin?

MARBLE:

Come now, Frank! Speak nicely to the gentleman.

> THE DUMMY *turns to* PABST.

THE DUMMY:

Good evening, Professor.

PABST:

Good evening, Frank.

> *He seats himself upon the bench at the
> foot of the little stage.* THE DUMMY *barks
> at him:*

THE DUMMY:

"*Mr.* Frenzy" to you, please!

PABST:

A thousand pardons.

THE DUMMY:

—Make it two thousand.

PABST:

Two thousand, then.

THE DUMMY:

I'll take it!

106

THE DUMMY *blinks its eyes and turns its empty face up to* MARBLE.

You seem depressed, Jim. What's the matter?

MARBLE:

Me? Depressed?

THE DUMMY:

Yeh—down in the mouth. What for?—Has the little witch been acting up again?

MARBLE:

The little—?—I don't know who you mean, Frank.

THE DUMMY:

W-i-t-c-h—"w" as in "butter." She certainly runs you ragged. I don't see how you stand it.

MARBLE:

If it's my wife you are referring to—

THE DUMMY:

Of course it's your wife! Who else would it be?

MARBLE:

I don't care to discuss my domestic affairs.

THE DUMMY:

You're going to whether you care to or not.

GERT *stirs in her chair.*

GERT:

Oh, lay off.

THE DUMMY'S *head swings in her direction.*

THE DUMMY:

Out! This is a private conversation—What a woman! Just a chippie off the old block, eh, Jim?

MARBLE:

To what block do you refer, Frank?

THE DUMMY:

Tenth Avenue, between Fourteenth and—

MARBLE:

—That's enough!

THE DUMMY:

It ought to be.

MARBLE:

You'd better learn not to be so outspoken, my friend.

THE DUMMY:

Hooey! The trouble with you is you never speak out. You let her get away with murder.

GERT:

Oh, he does, does he?—Look out, or there'll be a real one.

MARBLE:

I can't allow you to talk this way, Frank.

THE DUMMY:

Try and stop me.

MARBLE:

What are your views on politics? Do you think the Democrats—?

108

He takes a swallow of his drink. THE
DUMMY *talks through it:*

THE DUMMY:

I don't give a damn about politics! What worries
me is the ride that dame's taking you on.

MARBLE *puts down his glass.*

MARBLE:

My wife and I are very happy together, see?

THE DUMMY:

Like fun you are.

MARBLE:

She is the soul of loyalty—kind, generous, sweet-
tempered—

THE DUMMY:

Don't make me laugh.

MARBLE:

—Loving and economical. In fact, the perfect help-
meet.

THE DUMMY:

"Hell-cat," did you say?

GERT:

Thanks. That'll be about all!

MARBLE:

"Help-meet" is what I said.

THE DUMMY:

Hooey.

MARBLE:

I beg your pardon?

THE DUMMY:

Hooey! Hooey!

MARBLE:

Quiet, Frank—people will hear you.

THE DUMMY:

So they'd ought! All this secrecy—that's how she gets away with it. If everyone knew the way she—

> MARBLE *claps a hand over the mouth.*

MARBLE:

Insect!—Quiet, I say!

THE DUMMY:

Okay! Okay!

MARBLE:

Promise?

THE DUMMY:

Hope to die.

> MARBLE *removes his hand.* THE DUMMY *gasps, coughs once, and is quiet for a moment.*

GERT:

Very funny. In fact, a howl. I'll book you.

> MARBLE *lights a cigarette, keeping it in his mouth.*

MARBLE:

You know, Frank, sometimes you're almost as dumb as a man.

THE DUMMY:

Yep—and two women.

> MARBLE *offers the cigarette.*

MARBLE:

Would you like a smoke?

THE DUMMY:

No thanks. It gets in my eyes.

MARBLE:

Too bad.

THE DUMMY:

Yep—both of 'em.

MARBLE:

Do you care for bridge?

THE DUMMY:

Nope.

MARBLE:

Why not?

THE DUMMY:

I get tired of all the time being the dummy.

SPEEDY:

Marvelous! He's as good as Marshall Montgomery.

PABST:

—But this is extraneous. I feel the Truth struggling to come through. Something is holding it back—No?

HERE COME THE CLOWNS

> MARBLE *removes the cigarette from his*
> *mouth and puts it out, turning his head*
> *to one side with great deliberation as* THE
> DUMMY *turns in the opposite direction*
> *and gazes blankly into a space, attempting*
> *a whistle that does not quite come off.*
> *Finally it inquires disinterestedly:*

THE DUMMY:

Why are you such a liar, Jim?

MARBLE:

A liar? Me?

THE DUMMY:

Yes.—Why not out with the truth once in a while?
It would do you good—her, too.

MARBLE:

Truth is pretty dangerous medicine, old boy.

PABST:

—But effective—very often effective.

> THE DUMMY's *head swings around toward*
> *him.*

—I beg your pardon.

THE DUMMY:

I grant your grace. I hope the cat will spit in your
face.

PABST:

But are we not again departing from our subject?

112

MARBLE:

What subject is he referring to, Frank?

THE DUMMY:

You know: that little b-i-t—that little bit of a wife of yours.

> GERT *half rises.*

GERT:

I won't stand it!

THE DUMMY:

Then sit it!

MARBLE:

I'm afraid I'll have to ask you to mend your language, my friend.

THE DUMMY:

She's got her claws in you and she won't let go, will she?

MARBLE:

As a matter of fact, she's often told me I can leave any time I like.

GERT:

And I tell you again!

THE DUMMY:

Then why don't you?

MARBLE:

Why—I guess I just don't want to.

THE DUMMY:

More hooey—you mean you're too soft-hearted to.

You know if you don't watch her like a hawk she'll
go straight to hell in a hack—well, why not let her?

MARBLE:

> *After a moment.*

She was a sweet kid, once.

> *Then* MARBLE's *face changes, and* THE
> DUMMY *barks:*

THE DUMMY:

—You mean before the girls came around.

MARBLE:

The what?

THE DUMMY:

The girls! The girls! The girls!

> GERT *springs up.*

GERT:

What do you mean, you—!

> *The head swings around on her.*

THE DUMMY:

You heard me!—The girls!—The little ones—the
soft ones—the frilly ones—the girly-girls—

> GERT *advances threateningly.*

GERT:

I'll kill you, you damned little—

THE DUMMY:

And what do you call yourself?—What could sink
a man lower than to have to live with a woman
who—

GERT:

I won't stand it! I don't have to listen to such talk!
I—I'll—

> *She seizes* THE DUMMY *and shakes it vio‑*
> *lently.*

You—you foul little, lying little—

> *She flings it down and makes her way*
> *blindly to the restaurant door.*

You'll never see me again! Never in this world
—you hear me?

> *She is gone, the door banging closed after*
> *her.* MARBLE *picks up the sprawling*
> DUMMY, *replaces it in its black bag, pulls*
> *the strings together, hunches it into the*
> *crook of his arm and moves in the direc‑*
> *tion taken by* GERT. PABST *follows him.*

PABST:

Where are you going?

MARBLE:

After her. She'll just sit in there till I come.

PABST:

I would not, if I were you.

MARBLE:

Why not?

PABST:

Is that not just what she wants? Is that not just
what you always have done?

CONNIE:

But the poor. misguided creature—who else is she to turn to?

SPEEDY:

She's got a right to her own life!

DICKINSON:

Who says?

> MARBLE *stares at* PABST, *hesitates.* CLANCY
> *cries out.*

CLANCY:

Go on, Jim! Go on, man!

> MARBLE *turns and gazes at him. Finally*
> *he speaks:*

MARBLE:

No.

> *He sinks into a chair at the table, the black*
> *bag dropping at his feet.*

CLANCY:

—But she's your own wife!—And she might do some harm to herself.

MARBLE:

Let her! Who gives a damn?

CLANCY:

That's no thing to say!

PABST:

Wise—at last he grows wise.

116

CLANCY:

Wise, me foot! Who's to help her but him?

PABST:

Never mind her. The truth has set *him* free!

DICKINSON:

The hell it has. It's only moved him into another kind of prison.

MARBLE:

Shut up, the lot of you!

THE MAJOR:

You shouldn't have done it, Jim.

> PABST *turns blandly to* THE MAJOR.

PABST:

You, also, did not care for the performance?

THE MAJOR:

No, I did not.

PABST:

Perhaps you and I might give a better one—you think?

> THE MAJOR *stares at him.*

THE MAJOR:

How do you mean?

PABST:

You could be *my* little man—no?

THE MAJOR:

I don't understand you.

117

PABST:

Would you be so kind as to come on stage with me, please?

THE MAJOR:

No. No, thank you.

> PABST *moves closer to him, stands over him.*

PABST:

But I must insist! It is very important to a friend of yours—

> *He glances at* CLANCY.

—It is, in fact, essential.

SPEEDY:

Oh go on, Major—it's all in fun. Gracious!

THE MAJOR:

But I don't see how—

> PABST *holds a hand out to him.*

PABST:

Come—you will soon find out how. It is really as simple as what-you-say—a-b-c.

> *Reluctantly* THE MAJOR *takes the proffered hand and together they move to the rear of the room, mount the shallow steps and are upon the stage.*

SPEEDY:

The long and the short of it! Isn't it sweet?

118

PABST seats himself upon the chair that
MARBLE had occupied, swings THE MAJOR
around to him, lifts him up and sets him
upon his knee.

DICKINSON:

Do you see what I see?

SPEEDY:

Shh! No comments from the audience.

PABST:

Now then! Attention, please—everyone attention!
—Good evening, Major.

THE MAJOR:

Well, what is it you want to know from me?

PABST:

Just a few little things.—Like our friend Clancy,
there are small things that puzzle me.

THE MAJOR:

Well, what are they?

PABST:

We are a little world in ourselves, we vaudeville
artists, are we not?

THE MAJOR:

In a way, yes.—Yes, I expect we are.

PABST:

Our lives are so concentrated: twice a day, six days a
week, we must give our all in the brief space of ten
minutes.

THE MAJOR:

My act runs twenty.

PABST:

Twenty for the headliners—true. But we are not all headliners. Take our friend Clancy—he is hardly one of us at all—and yet, he, too, is a kind of essence. Wouldn't you say?

THE MAJOR:

Yes. Yes, I would. Very much of a one.

PABST:

And at present seems to believe that he represents, in his small self, all the essential troubles of the world.

CLANCY:

I never said—!

PABST:

Move nearer, Mr. Clancy.

> *With a downward, sweeping motion of his arm he invites him to them.*

Sit here at our feet, that you may be even more one of us.

> CLANCY *comes forward and seats himself upon the second step of the stage-steps.*

CLANCY:

I don't know at all what it is that you're after—

PABST:

Only the Truth, Mr. Clancy. The ways there, alas, are not always straight ways.

> *He turns again to the* MAJOR, *urging him.*

Tell me about this Clancy. Acquaint me briefly with the facts of his decline and his fall.

CLANCY:

That might be private.

PABST:

Quiet, please.

> THE MAJOR *speaks woodenly.*

THE MAJOR:

From the beginning, his life has been a hard one. As a boy he knew cold and hunger, and he has known them since.—He never asked for much, and much was never given him.

CLANCY:

Don't make me out sorry for myself now—for I'm not!

THE MAJOR:

—In fact, the little that he had, at last was taken from him. He lost his little home and he lost his little savings. He lost the sight of one eye.

CLANCY:

Well, I never did any crying over myself with either of them. It's not such things alone—

121

THE MAJOR:

—He lost his job—his young brother and his little daughter. That was the worst. He was left with only his beloved wife to mourn all these things that had been so dear to him. Then he woke one fine morning and found that she was gone too.

PABST:

His wife? Where to? With whom—a lover?

CLANCY *springs up*.

CLANCY:

Put up your dukes! You get a poke in the nose for that!

PABST *holds his hands out to him*.

PABST:

Forgive me—

CLANCY:

Then why did you say such a thing?

PABST:

I was in error: forgive me.

CLANCY:

The poor child left me because she thought she was bad luck for me. She said it to me once: "I bring you bad luck, Dan," she said.

PABST:

Of course—of course—

CLANCY:

—"Of course" no such thing! She only thought it!

122

PABST:

I understand.

CLANCY:

See that you do!—And in the future, mind your tongue.

> PABST *bows his head.* CLANCY *reseats himself.* PABST *turns again to* THE MAJOR.

PABST:

—And his little girl—how old was she?

THE MAJOR:

I don't know precisely. Two—three—

CLANCY:

Three years, four months, two days.

PABST:

They are sweet at that age.

CLANCY:

She was!—And she was good, too, and pretty as a picture and full of jokes and laughing. Never a tear out of her, except now and then when her little insides hurt her, with the wind or the like—or when she grew aware of the vast world about her and felt too small in it and needed comforting.

PABST:

—A bitter blow to lose her.

CLANCY:

It was, that. How it happened, I don't know—or why it ever did. She was always well and strong,

123

for all that she was a seven months' baby. It started with no more than a little cold—the same as any child might have in changing weather. But it grew and it grew until it was all the way through her and then the doctor could only shake his head and sit and watch her, fighting for breath, beating her little fists in the air.

PABST:

What could be sadder?

CLANCY:

There's little that could be.—I don't know of anything could, now I think of it.—Angela was all that was ever all my own. My job could be taken any time—the eye is a delicate organ, subject to accidents—my house was never fully paid for—young Timmy, my brother, drank—and my Nora was my wife only so long as she was willing to put up with me. But Angela was all my own.

PABST:

Still, all such deprivations mean something—don't you agree, Major? They all have some purpose in the scheme of life.

DICKINSON:

Oh, sure, sure—they add zest.

CLANCY:

But mean *what?* That's what I want to know! The purpose of 'em!—And I want to know other things!

PABST:

Would you wish to have had a child, too, Major?

THE MAJOR'S face sets.

THE MAJOR:

I had one.

PABST seems surprised.

PABST:

Indeed.

THE MAJOR:

Yes, I had a son.

PABST:

That was long ago—

THE MAJOR:

Yes—that was long ago.

PABST:

After a moment.

And where is he now?

THE MAJOR:

I can't say. I don't know.

PABST:

Tell us a little, Major. Speak out to us. It will do you good.

> *There is a brief silence. Then THE MAJOR'S voice begins, toneless and flat, as if reading faded print aloud:*

THE MAJOR:

Anna and I had wanted a child for years, but we had been afraid. We—

He stops again. PABST *helps him:*

PABST:

She was small, too, I take it.

THE MAJOR:

—Smaller even than me. She could walk under my arm. That's the way she came on stage with me: it made a—it made a very good entrance. She was the only grown-up I have ever known that I was bigger than. She was a true midget, not a dwarf like me—fine in every part—hands, feet, little wrists and ankles, all perfectly proportioned. She had the bluest eyes ever there were—my, they were blue! She was a treat to see. A reviewer in Savannah once referred to her as "the Vest-pocket Venus" and other papers took it up. Finally we used it in our billing: "Major Armstrong and His Vest-pocket Venus."

PABST:

Charming.—And the child?

THE MAJOR:

We—we thought that having one would be like shouting from the housetops, "Look! See how these small people have loved! Love is not denied the small in stature if their souls, if their spirits be—"

Again he stops and swallows. Then he goes on:

—He was born as Caesar was, and the medical men in attendance were very interested and very pleased with themselves. He was—all right in every way— like Anna's grandmother—like my father.

SPEEDY:

Who'd ever believe such a thing! Gracious!

PABST:

But were you not gratified?

THE MAJOR:

At first, yes—we were even proud of it. But finally, as he kept growing, it got so that we couldn't sleep at night, wondering, planning, fearing. At four he was as tall as his mother was. At five, he came to here on me. We were—we were like three children together.—But when he was seven, we sent him away.

PABST:

—For his own good. An unselfish and noble act.

THE MAJOR:

—All I know is, that try as she might my Anna could not endure a world without him. Month by month she dwindled away to nothing and one night she just turned on her pillow and died.

PABST:

Dear, dear, how dreadful.

127

THE MAJOR:

It was here, in the Sims' Hotel. I would have followed her, but Mr. Concannon gave me the courage to wait.

PABST:

James Concannon?

THE MAJOR:

Is there another?

PABST:

—And what became of the boy?

THE MAJOR:

The people he was with were not good people—they couldn't have been, because he ran away from them. I've never been able to find out where—or anything about him—though I've tried very hard to.

> *He looks away.*

He'd be a grown man now. I—I daresay he'd make a dozen of me.

> *He waits an instant, then looks up at*
> PABST.

—And now may I get down, please?

PABST:

One moment.

> *He turns to* CLANCY.

Well, Mr. Clancy—?

> CLANCY *looks up. His eyes are dazed again.*

CLANCY:

Who—? Where—? What did you say?

> PABST *turns to the others.*

PABST:

—It appears that our saddened friend does not yet realize that others among us also have our burdens to bear.

CLANCY:

Ah, that I do! I do indeed! But what help is that to anyone?

> *He turns to* THE MAJOR.

My heart is knotted up into a fist for you, Major.

THE MAJOR:

Thank you, Clancy.

> PABST *frowns down upon* CLANCY.

PABST:

Which is the worse—to have the Almighty take a child, or to have to give it away to strangers? To have it safe in heaven—or to have it roam the world, nameless and alone?

CLANCY:

The cases are not the same—nor the circumstances! But both are bad, both!

PABST:

Which is the better—to have one's wife die, wracked to the bone with grief—or to have her leave one, and live on?

129

CLANCY:

It's not the same—there's no similarity!

> *There is a pause.* PABST *ponders, then turns and speaks suddenly:*

PABST:

You, there—Cooper and Farrel—

> *They start in surprise. He adds, softly:*

Would you come a little nearer, please?

> LEW *and* FAY *look at each other uncertainly, then rise.*

You, Miss—another step forward—one, two, three!

> *Deliberately* FAY *advances three steps, and three only.*

Now, then, little song-and-dance lady—hearing what you have heard, do you still wish to marry?

> FAY *replies stoutly:*

FAY:

Yes. I do.

PABST:

And have a child—children?

FAY:

Yes. I do!

LEW:

Look: what's the idea?

PABST:

So young, so brave, so unafraid. Is it not interestin', Major? Is it not interestin', Mr. Clancy?

They do not reply. He turns to FAY *again,
smiling his smile.*

Pretty as you are, it should be so simple—just to
take him by the hand and lead him to the altar—no?

FAY:

Maybe it should be, but it's not.

PABST:

And why, pray?

FAY:

He won't come.

PABST:

He must have his reasons.

FAY:

I suppose he has. But he keeps them to himself.

PABST:

Dear, dear.—Are you quite sure he loves you?

FAY:

Yes. Yes, I am.

LEW:

What *is* this? Why should you have to tell this old
goat what you—

PABST:

"Old goat"? That is not nice. That is not nice at
all.

131

LEW:

> *Advancing.*

Oh, can it! What right have you got to mix in, anyway?

PABST:

> That's it—closer. Come a little closer.
>> LEW *stops abruptly.*

LEW:

> I'll stay where I am, thanks.

PABST:

> But this is impolite of you. It is not in the interests of a varied entertainment.
>> *He coaxes and smiles, gesturing:*
> Come, young man—come—come—

LEW:

> That'll be all right!

PABST:

> He is stubborn, little Major. It appears *we* must go to *him.*
>> *With* THE MAJOR *perched awkwardly against his shoulder he proceeds down the stage steps, advances to* LEW *and stands directly facing him.*
> Look at him, little Major. Gaze upon this strange contradiction: a young man in love who will not marry. Talented, well-off, sound in limb and in sinew, and still he will not marry.

LEW:

That's my business, isn't it?

PABST:

Ah yes—deeply so. Look at him, Major—you are a wise little man—perhaps you can account for this perverse attitude. All that we know of him is that he is a foundling, that he is in love and that he will not marry.—Ah, yes! And one thing more—

LEW:

Shut up. Shut up, you!

PABST:

—Just one—a certain unaccountable distaste for very small people, like yourself. Look at him closer—consider the brow, the elevated cheek-bones. And the eyes—did you ever see eyes so blue in a man's head? Where have you ever seen their like before?

> LEW *begins to tremble. His hands close*
> *and unclose spasmodically.*

He seems to grow nervous—I wonder why? Of what can he be afraid?

> *His voice lowers.*

Little Major—does it not grow more apparent why he will not marry?

> *A sudden cry is wrung from* THE MAJOR
> *and he turns his gaze sharply from the*
> *dancer's face. But* PABST *goes on:*

133

Is it not now somewhat more evident who he is?

> THE MAJOR *struggles in* PABST'S *arms.*

LEW:

You—you fishy, fat-headed slob, you—what the hell
do you think you're trying to pull off?

THE MAJOR:

Let me go! Let me go!

PABST:

—But certainly.

> *He sets him carefully down upon his feet.*
> THE MAJOR *totters toward the stage, sinks
> down upon the lowest step and sits there,
> his head in his hands, his narrow shoulders
> shaking.* FAY *looks wonderingly from him
> to* LEW, *then back again.*

FAY:

Oh Lew—

> *Suddenly* LEW *shouts:*

LEW:

He lies! He's not!

> PABST *inquires mildly:*

PABST:

Who is not what? Have I said anything?

LEW:

Plenty! But it's not true I'm his—he's my—!—And
you know damn well it's not!

134

PABST:

Of course, of course—

LEW:

Then why do you make it seem that it is? You, with your oily roundabout way of—your cheap, ten-twenty-thirty trick of piling it up, and then making it sound like it was the McCoy—!

He flounders and stops.

FAY:

Lew—listen, Lew—

LEW:

I tell you it's just his rotten idea of being funny! It's a stinking lie, the whole thing, cooked-up out of nothing! I'll be damned if I'll hang around and take any more of it! To hell with the lot of you—

He storms out into the alley. CLANCY *drops down upon the step and throws one arm protectingly about* THE MAJOR. FAY *moves to the alley-door, where she turns and faces* PABST.

FAY:

I think—I think you're a living horror. God damn you to hell.

She goes out. PABST *sighs, lowers his head and clasps his hands across his front.*

135

PABST:

Dear, dear. It seems that even the semblance of Truth is not popular.

CLANCY:

The "semblance," is it? Then you're admitting yourself it's not so!

PABST:

We always have coincidence to contend with.

CONNIE:

—And "coincidence," too—it's a grand time to be saying that!

PABST:

I regret I have not your command of the language.

CONNIE:

And don't be coming at us with that kind of five-act talk! Even if it was a fact, facts aren't the truth always.

PABST:

Now there—*there* you have me. That is very astute of you.

DICKINSON:

Why should we take all this from you, anyhow?

PABST:

Shall I stop where I am, perhaps?

136

DICKINSON:

Hell, no. We've seen nothing yet that any small-time ham couldn't pull off as well or better.

PABST *looks at him oddly.*

PABST:

Thank you. Then I shall proceed.

DICKINSON:

In the interests of accuracy, it just happens that *I* know who Lew's father is—and where he is.

CLANCY:

Then tell him, man, tell him!

DICKINSON:

I'd sooner draw and quarter him.

SPEEDY:

Is it that bad?

DICKINSON:

It's worse.

PABST *is looking at* DICKINSON *with new interest. He crooks his finger at him and murmurs mockingly.*

PABST:

Ah-ha!

DICKINSON *gestures him away.*

CLANCY:

After a moment.

Anyhow, Major, now you know it's not so, not a bit of it.

137

THE MAJOR:

All I know is that if ever I did find him, it might—
it might be like that.

CLANCY *glances angrily at* PABST.

CLANCY:

You tricky old wretch, you. Lew and Fay were
better off as they were—and so was the Major.

PABST:

—But advise me seriously, Mr. Clancy—would you
not rather your daughter were dead than that she
had ever grown up to deny you?

CLANCY:

She never would have!

CONNIE:

Why should she have? Where's the girl ever had a
better man for a father?

CLANCY:

And I say again, you shouldn't have done this to
the Major. You've not done him good, you've done
him ill!

PABST:

A matter of opinion.—Would you rather it had
been done to you?

CLANCY:

There's nothing can be done to me any more! All
that could be, has been.

138

PABST:

Are you sure?

CLANCY:

I am.

PABST:

That must console you.

CLANCY:

I have other consolations.

PABST:

Ah? Such as—

CLANCY:

I had a wife who loved me once, and still does maybe. I had a good job to occupy my mind. I had my health and I had a small house with a flower-bed behind it. And for a time I had a little girl who was all my own. I had everything!

PABST:

Brave memories.

CLANCY:

There'll never be braver! They're of a nature to comfort any man alive!—But as for you, I can't for the life of me figure you out. What are you up to with all these cooney tricks, anyhow? Why do you do what you do?

PABST:

Perhaps at heart I am a humanitarian.

CONNIE:

At what?—I doubt if you've got one.—Come along, Dan, you can sleep at Mrs. Carlson's. She's got an empty bed.

CLANCY:

Yes—I'll come—

He turns again to PABST.

—Good night to you, old sly-boots, and small thanks, if any.

PABST:

So—you give up your great search so easily.

CLANCY:

You can leave that to me!

PABST:

—You hug your "consolations" to you, and settle for a penny in the pound. Most interestin', most.

DICKINSON *thumps upon the table.*

DICKINSON:

Connemara—to Connemara!

CLANCY *glances at him, then back to* PABST.

PABST:

No—it is too difficult. The Irish are a soft race, really. The bravery is all in front.

CLANCY:

Who says it is?

140

CONNIE:

Dan—here we go, Dan—

CLANCY:

No. Wait a bit.

> *To* PABST.

Who says they are?

PABST:

—An Irishman without a cause—is there a sadder sight in the world?

CLANCY:

If my cause is a lost one, it's none the less my own, you old crock!

PABST:

—One moment, please.

> *In the center of the room he deftly ar-*
> *ranges two chairs, facing each other.*
> *Then he moves quickly to* SPEEDY, *bends*
> *and whispers something to him.* SPEEDY
> *looks at him blankly. Now* PABST *speaks*
> *aloud to him:*

Please not to make difficulties. Tell her it is only for a moment. Tell her he has gone—

> SPEEDY *hesitates briefly, then goes to the*
> *restaurant door and out.* CLANCY *seats*
> *himself stubbornly in the chair with its*
> *back to the door.* CONNIE *advances to him.*

CONNIE:

Well, are you coming or aren't you?

CLANCY:

Sit down a bit, Connie.

CONNIE:

I will not.

PABST *approaches them.*

CLANCY:

Why not? Just one little minute, till—

CONNIE:

Because that's what he wants us to do! And I'll tell him nothing!

PABST:

What is there to tell?

CONNIE:

You heard me, didn't you?—Nothing!

PABST:

No?—Not one little word to the one man in the whole world you—

CONNIE:

—That isn't so! I don't! I don't at all!

PABST:

—Don't what? What have I said?

CONNIE:

Never mind!—Come on, Dan. I don't like it here. I don't like it a bit. I've got a queer feeling it's— well, what are you looking at me so funny for?

142

He is gazing at her, his eyes again dazed, as if he had found something gravely amiss.

Are you coming or are you not?

CLANCY:

What's different about your face, Connie? What's wrong with it?

CONNIE:

Nothing that hasn't always been. You don't have to look at it!

CLANCY:

I know!—Where are your earrings?

CONNIE:

I never had earrings.

CLANCY:

You did so. Your grandmother pierced your ears with a hot needle when you were small and she set little round gold earrings in them and said you'd never get the rheumatism.

CONNIE:

She did no such thing!

CLANCY:

You told me she did.

CONNIE:

You're thinking of Nora.

> *A moment, then* CLANCY's *head droops and he murmurs.*

CLANCY:

So I am. So I am.

CONNIE:

I wouldn't have them on a bet.

CLANCY:

They're pretty things.

CONNIE:

—Not if I had to die for the lack of them, I wouldn't.

CLANCY:

You were always the stubborn one, Connie.

CONNIE:

Be that as it may, I—!

> *She stops suddenly and gazes in alarm beyond him to the opposite side of the room where* NORA *stands in the doorway,* SPEEDY *behind her.* CONNIE *speaks softly:*

—Take it easy, Dan. You're in for it now, all right.

> *Curtain*

HERE COME THE CLOWNS

ACT III

ACT III

The Same.

The positions are the same as at the end of Act Two. The time is immediately after it. The action is continuous.

SPEEDY *is urging* NORA *into the room.*

SPEEDY:

Just a little informal entertainment, that's all.

NORA:

But why should I be the stooge for a trick-man, for God's sake? The gentleman I'm with steps into the washroom for a minute, and—

> CLANCY *straightens abruptly at the sound of her voice, but does not turn.* PABST *holds the chair opposite him out for* NORA.

PABST:

—This way, Madam, if you will be so good.

> *She moves uncertainly past* CLANCY *to the chair.*

NORA:

But what's the point? My friend won't know where I've—

> *She turns, sees* CLANCY, *and gasps:*

You!

She grasps the back of the chair.

Speedy said you'd gone. He said—

CLANCY:

Nora—

Then suddenly he springs up, crying out joyously:

Ah, Nora, Nora—you've come back!

And moves swiftly toward her. NORA *draws herself erect against the chair.*

NORA:

I have not! And you stay where you are—keep your distance away from me!

CLANCY *stops in his tracks and gazes at her.*

Go back where you were.

He does not move.

I mean it!—Don't you know yet that I mean what I say?

Dumbly CLANCY *returns to his chair.* NORA *turns and meets* CONNIE'S *accusing eyes, with dark resentment in her own.*

I suppose it's you I've got to thank for this.

CONNIE:

I'd nothing to do with it. I'd've done wonders to keep it off.

NORA *seats herself with deliberation, faces* CLANCY *squarely and demands:*

148

NORA:

Well—what do you want?

> CLANCY *can only stare.* DICKINSON *waits*
> *a moment, then speaks.*

DICKINSON:

I suppose we just might have the decency to clear
out and leave them.

MARBLE:

I was thinking that.

THE MAJOR:

Yes.

NORA:

What for? This is a free-for-all. The more the mer-
rier.

> *She turns again to* CLANCY.

Well—get it out, can't you? I left a good plate of
eggs for this.

CLANCY:

You're changed.

NORA:

Only to you, I imagine.

CLANCY:

You were never like this.

NORA:

I was always like this.

CLANCY:

No—you've got hard.

NORA:

I was born hard, hard as nails.

CLANCY:

I never saw it.

NORA:

You weren't let: I took good care of that.

CLANCY *frowns at her, puzzled.*

CLANCY:

What is it you're saying? What is it you mean?

NORA:

You had such a sweet little idea of me, I thought
I'd live up to it, that's all.

CLANCY:

I don't believe it.

NORA:

You never believe anything but what you want to.

CLANCY:

And that's not so, either.

NORA:

It is, and everything I'll be telling you will be!
That's why I'm willing to sit here, to put you
straight once and for all—so you'll never trouble
me again, ever.

CLANCY:

"Trouble" you, did you say?

150

NORA:

That's what I said. You're a blight on me, Dan Clancy, and you always have been.

CLANCY:

This can't be you, Nora. Surely it can't.

NORA:

But it is.

CLANCY:

You who were so good and gentle and loving—

NORA:

I know!—I ought to of gone on the stage.

CLANCY:

Something's just suddenly come over you. Tell me, so I can—

NORA:

Oh, tie it outside! You're a worse fool than I thought you.

CLANCY *half rises.*

CLANCY:

You mind your tongue, Miss!

NORA:

—Irish.—It doesn't scare me. It never did. I was raised on it.

CLANCY *turns in bewilderment to* CONNIE.

CLANCY:

What's the matter with her, Connie? What is it?

CONNIE:

She's had a drink or two, I guess. Dutch courage, I guess.

NORA:

You keep your oar out!

CLANCY:

But she never touched anything.

NORA:

Oh didn't I? And didn't I used to have a fine laugh at you, for not catching on!

CLANCY:

You've been bewitched.

> *She leans toward him, elbow on knee, chin on hand, exasperated.*

NORA:

Listen—will you never learn?

CLANCY:

Why did you run away from me with never a word? Was it because of all the misfortune that had suddenly come on us—and you thinking you'd brought it?

NORA:

That's what you told yourself, is it?

CLANCY:

I'm asking you, Nora—and what's more, you're to tell me.

152

NORA:

That was part of it, yes.

CLANCY:

What else?

NORA:

Because I couldn't stand you!
> *He looks at her aghast.*

CLANCY:

You don't mean that all at once there was no more love in your heart for me—

NORA:

I mean there never was any!
> CLANCY *frowns, still unable to comprehend. Again he turns to* CONNIE.

CLANCY:

She's joking.—You hear her, Connie: she's trying to make some kind of a joke.

NORA:

Joke, my eye! I'm saying what I mean now, for once—and I mean just that—never ever—never a scrap of love!
> *He looks at her from under his brows.*

CLANCY:

For nearly four years we were man and wife—

NORA:

You don't need to tell *me* that!

CLANCY:

—You can't fool me, Nora. I have too good a memory.

> *She sees what he means, and laughs shortly.*

NORA:

Oh, I liked that part of it all right. I got round heels, you know.

> CLANCY's *face sets and his now angered eyes travel her from head to foot and back again. Finally he speaks very softly.*

CLANCY:

—From a dear and a loving and warm-hearted girl, full of grace and delight, something or someone has turned you in no time at all into a cheap, dirty-mouthed little piece. Someone has put a spell on you—who is it?

NORA:

So there has to be someone *else*, does there? Listen, you—

CLANCY:

Who is it? Tell me who it is. Because I'll render him null and void, so I will!

NORA:

Don't be a fool. No one's anything to me but myself, and never has been.

154

CONNIE:

That's nice of you. It's right sweet of you to leave him something.

> CLANCY *looks from one to the other, then rises and goes to* NORA, *stands over her, searching the impudent pretty face for something he wants desperately to find there. At last he speaks.*

CLANCY:

It's not that I don't love and cherish you as I always have, but you anger me. Your unwomanly talk and your vast impertinences and the silly, hollowed-out sound of a laugh that used to be sweet like a string-orchestra—it makes me angry.

NORA:

So what?

CLANCY:

I don't know yet, but you must be made to un-learn your new tricks.

NORA:

Oh? By who?

CLANCY:

By me!—You fresh, brassy little jape, sitting there on your hard seat with that new chippie look in your shoe-button eyes and that two-for-a-dollar smile round your mouth, you were once my wife, you still are. And I'll have no wife of mine abroad on such behavior, and you can make book on it!

NORA:

So what do you plan to do?

CLANCY:

You know what I'd like to do this minute?—I'd like to give you one with the flat of me hand that'd send you spinning down the Ages.

NORA:

—Only you won't.

CLANCY:

Don't be so sure, Miss.

NORA:

You haven't it in you to. You're the original Mister Softheart, and your hands were made for love-pats.

> *She rises.*

Well—save 'em for someone else. I'm not taking any.

> *She drops a step or two back from him, opens her handbag, peers into a mirror in it, puts powder on her nose, snaps the bag shut and addresses him with a fine air of finality.*

Anything more?—If not, I'll be getting along now.

CLANCY:

You will, will you?

NORA:

Yes I will.

CLANCY:

You'll stay directly where you are! You'll not move a step till I've found out another thing or two.

NORA:

You're the thorough one, aren't you? Just a real good housecleaning.

CLANCY:

There's many the dirty chimney I'd like to send the goose down tonight, I can tell you that!

> *She turns to* SPEEDY *with a great show of dignity.*

NORA:

Mr. Speedy, is it customary for ladies to be detained in your place against their wish?

SPEEDY:

I never come between husband and wife. I've learned enough for—

> *He stops as the door from the restaurant is opened and* GURNEY *comes in. He is lighting a cigarette and kicks the door to after him.*

GURNEY:

Hello, everybody. How about a round on me?

Silence greets him. He looks up, puzzled, and snaps his cigarette lighter shut with a flourish as CLANCY *turns slowly and regards him. He tosses the lighter into the air, catches it again, pockets it and casually advances into the room.*

How are you, Clancy, old man? We've missed you round the Globe. It hasn't been the same place without your daily Specialty. How about a small one on me, to celebrate the homecoming?

CLANCY:

No thank you.

GURNEY:

No?—Then how about—er—your good lady?

CLANCY:

She neither.

PABST:

—Isn't it interestin'?

GURNEY:

Your eye looks fine—damned if I'd know it was any different from the other.

CLANCY:

Never mind my eye!

GURNEY:

Oh, come on! What's all the gloom about? Lent's over!

158

CLANCY:

I wish you would go.

GURNEY:

Thanks for the buggy-ride, only I'm staying.

CLANCY:

I wish you would kindly leave now.

GURNEY:

You're kidding. You know I'm a permanent attraction here.

> *He seats himself at* DICKINSON's *table and slaps his hand down upon it.*

Come on—fill 'em up!

> *He fills a glass from the whisky bottle and looks about him.*

What! No music? Where's Piano Mary?

> CLANCY *leans back against the table. Again his eyes have the dazed look in them.*

CLANCY:

Maybe I'm hungry. I don't know when I ate last.

> CONNIE *rises.*

CONNIE:

I'll bring something in for you from the Front.

> CLANCY *straightens.*

CLANCY:

No. I don't want it.

> *Again he turns and addresses* GURNEY.

I ask you please to move along out of here. I'm talking with my wife.

> GURNEY *squints through his glass at the others.*

GURNEY:

I see: just a private run-through with all the boxes full. Why pick on me?

CLANCY:

I don't like you, Val Gurney, and I never did. All I ever owed you was that it was through you that I first met up with Nora. But since she's left me I owe you no more.

GURNEY:

Why, Clancy, you surprise me. I thought we were old friends. What's the trouble between you and the Missus?

> CLANCY *looks at* NORA.

CLANCY:

It turns out it was a stray cat I brought home. I buttered her paws, but she stayed only to lick them off, and then strayed again.

GURNEY:

You don't say. And I thought you'd be the perfect match.

CLANCY:

I remember you said so.

Suddenly he advances to NORA *and seizes her wrist.*

Only where did you stray *to?*

NORA:

Let go!

CLANCY:

I never thought—but I'm thinking now! Who was it?

CONNIE:

Go easy, Dan.

NORA:

You let me go!

CLANCY:

Tell me his name! I'll—!

>   NORA *cries out for help.*

NORA:

Val! Val!

>   CLANCY *drags her up to him and stares into her face, then thrusts her aside and gazes incredulously at* GURNEY. PABST *whispers something to* SPEEDY, *and unnoticed by the others, they move to the restaurant door and go out.* GURNEY *puts out his cigarette and rises uncertainly.*

GURNEY:

Look here, old man—no need for any rough stuff, you know.

CLANCY:

—So it was you.

GURNEY:

Never mind about that. The point now is—

CLANCY:

Never mind about it?

GURNEY:

What I mean is, we can settle everything peace-fully, with no hard feelings.

CLANCY:

Settle a man's wife running off from him to another man—and one the likes of you?

GURNEY:

Let's not get personal, now.

MARBLE:

What would you like him to get?

DICKINSON:

Yes—*you* tell us, will you?

GURNEY:

Keep out, the lot of you! This is between Clancy and me. Am I right, Dan?

CLANCY:

It is, that. It is surely.

GURNEY:

It could happen to any of us, you know. What a man wants with a woman he can't hold, I could never see anyway.

162

CLANCY:

Couldn't you?

GURNEY:

No, frankly I couldn't.

CLANCY:

And why?

GURNEY:

Well, it's—you know—just bad box-office. It's bound to flop sooner or later.

CONNIE:

Oh, the worm!

> CLANCY *advances.*

GURNEY:

Keep away!—If you so much as touch me, I'll—
> *But* CLANCY'S *hand is at the back of his neck now, and has begun to shake him slowly, like a sack.* GURNEY *struggles to free himself from the grasp, gasping:*

Let go, you fool! What do you think you're doing?

NORA:

Stop it! Stop!
> *But the shaking goes on.*

GURNEY:

You, Speedy—call somebody! What kind of a joint is this?

NORA:

Oh, stop it! Stop! Stop!

163

CONNIE:

He had it coming. You both of you had.

> *With one twist of his arm,* CLANCY *sends*
> GURNEY *crashing against the base of the*
> *little stage, where he lies for a moment*
> *before he finds his feet again. Finally he*
> *rises, pulls himself together, brushes him-*
> *self off, eyeing* CLANCY *with a look half*
> *fear, half hatred. He makes his way to the*
> *alley-door. His hand fumbles behind him*
> *for the door knob, finds it, turns it and*
> *holds on to it. Then he spits out his words:*

GURNEY:

You scum. You half-witted moron. Come around
and ask me some more questions sometime. Ask me
about your kid, for instance. She came pretty quick,
didn't she?—Seven months, my foot—six was nearer
it! Why else do you think Nora married you, you
poor, dumb—

CONNIE:

No, no!

> NORA *breaks in frantically:*

NORA:

Don't listen to him!

> CLANCY *strides toward* GURNEY *but he is*
> *out the door before he can reach him.*

NORA *stands shaking with rage, muttering to herself:*

He's lying. He's—

CLANCY *comes up behind her.*

CLANCY:

Then why did you marry me—and not him?
He swings her around to him.
Tell me!

CONNIE:

Don't hurt her, Dan!

CLANCY:

She'll tell me!—Why?

NORA:

He—he wouldn't. However much I asked—however much I—

CLANCY:

It was him introduced us, him that brought us together. And from the first sight of you, you knew it was all up with me. And you took me straight off—

NORA:

He made me! He kept after me till I—

CLANCY:

—You put your head on my shoulder and said, "Let's not wait, Dan. Let's not wait a week even." Do you remember you did?

NORA:

You don't know—you don't know—

CLANCY:

That was in April—and less than seven months after —on the second day of November—though we'd not looked for it till the first of the year, if that soon—and the doctor said often at seven months if the mother was not as strong as she might be—

> *Suddenly his voice catches and he stops. His head drops upon his breast. He murmurs to himself:*

—And I told myself there was no more ill could happen to me!

> *He raises his head, his face working. He touches her once, twice, lightly upon the shoulder with two fingers, speaking very gently.*

—You can go along now, Nora.

> *He takes her coat from the chair and lays it upon her shoulders, pulling it awkwardly into place.*

There now—there we are.

> *The pressure of his hand directs her to the door. He holds it open for her.*

Good-by now. When I think of the frets and the worries you've had, my heart aches for you, you bad girl, you.—Good-by, now. Good-by, Nora—

166

She turns and looks at him. Finally she speaks.

NORA:

Don't hate me, Dan.

CLANCY:

No, Nora—no.

She goes out and he closes the door after her. He stands there for a moment, then squares his shoulders, comes up to the table where THE MAJOR *and* DICKINSON *sit and takes the chair left by* MA SPEEDY.

I think I'll have a small drink now, if that's agreeable.

DICKINSON fills a glass and sets it before him. He drains it at a gulp, puts it down and draws the back of his hand across his mouth.

—That's what I needed.—"There comes a time," as they say.

DICKINSON:

Oh yes, it's a swell world. God's in His Heaven, all right—and He's going to stay there.

This time CLANCY *makes no attempt to refute him. He stares down at the table and his fingers begin to drum on it.* CONNIE *slips into the chair beside him, catches at the hand and holds it flat between her*

167

> *two own, rubbing it back and forth, as if
> to draw the blood back into it.*

CONNIE:

She was yours, little Angela was. She was all your own. Never have I known a baby to go so for any man. You were the one bright star in her little life. She was just a little fool for you, Dan—no one else even counted with her.

> *He swings around, frees his hand and joyously opens and shuts it between his face and* CONNIE's. *His eyes are bright with tears, though he is half-laughing. He demands of her:*

CLANCY:

D'you remember—? How she—how she used to—? The way she would—?—When I'd come in before supper and she heard my tread on the stairs, how she'd—?

> *He cannot finish.* CONNIE's *arm goes around his shoulders, contracts briefly and is withdrawn.*

CONNIE:

She was all yours. She was all your own.

> CLANCY *shakes his head slowly.*

CLANCY:

She was not—and Nora never was neither. And all my fine consolations are no more than a heap of

168

angel-droppings, as my young brother Tim used to say.

CONNIE:

Hush, Dan—

Suddenly he strikes his fist upon the table.

CLANCY:

I'll not! There's too much hushing done! We hush when we should be—!

He throws back his head and shouts:

—You up there, why do You send such blank confusion upon the world? What's the earthly good of half the things that happen?—Things that on the face of them are blundering injustices with no sense nor purpose—what's the reason for them?

He drags himself to his feet and half-circles the room.

Have You not said You'd come when we called You? Then where are You keeping Yourself?— What have You to lose by passing a moment or two with a man of Your own making in such unholy need of You?

His arm lashes through the air in a peremptory gesture and his voice thunders the command:

Can You not hear me? Then come to me! Come!

There is an expectant moment, as if the others half-believed the command would

> *be obeyed. Then* DICKINSON's *glass upon the table shatters the silence.*

DICKINSON:

Knock, and it shall be locked in your face. Seek, and you'll go on seeking.

CLANCY:

Don't say it. Never say such a thing.

MARBLE:

It's a sell, Dan, see?—All we can do is to make the best of it.

THE MAJOR:

—That's what I say—the best of it.

CONNIE:

It's—it's a long way up to heaven, you know—and it's a long way down.

CLANCY:

It's a long time here—that I know, I know that.

DICKINSON:

—*Now* do you believe in Him?

CLANCY:

I don't know where He keeps Himself.

DICKINSON:

Because your only hope is not to, Clancy. Anyone's is.

> CONNIE *goes to* CLANCY *and takes his hand in hers.*

170

CONNIE:

Don't mind him. Don't mind anything. Come along, now. It's sleep you need, Dan.

CLANCY:

It is, it is that.

CONNIE:

—And maybe it's a better day tomorrow, you know.

CLANCY:

Yesterday was the good day—yesterday a long time ago.

> *He stands for a moment, staring dully at the floor, then kicks at it once, as if to remove a worthless object from his path.*

What good is the Truth when you don't know what to do with it?

DICKINSON:

Don't tell me it hasn't set *you* free, either.

> CLANCY *moves toward the alley with* CONNIE, *mumbling:*

CLANCY:

Free for what? Free for what?

> *Suddenly, through the spangled curtains at the back of the little stage a light is seen.* CLANCY *stops at the sight of it. Then the curtains are opened quietly, and from the now open private doorway there emerges the figure of an old man in a gray*

*suit. He wears a soft white shirt with a
flowing black tie. He has a gray mustache
and his head is crowned with a great shock
of white hair. He wears spectacles, and
although his features are somewhat blurred
against the strong light from the staircase
behind him, it can be seen that his face is
kindly, even benevolent. There is a white
carnation in his buttonhole. He comes a
few steps forward upon the stage and
stands looking down over it, into the room.*
THE MAJOR *looks up with a start and
catches his breath.*

THE MAJOR:

It's—it's Mr.—!

All follow his eyes. When THE FIGURE
*speaks, it is in a thin, musical Irish voice,
the accent much broader than* CLANCY'S.

THE FIGURE:

Dan Clancy—

CLANCY *turns slowly.* THE FIGURE *smiles
down at him, his face growing suddenly
almost youthful with the smile.*

—Don't be in such a hurry, Clancy.

CLANCY:

Mr. Concannon!—Look, Connie—it's Mr. Concannon!

CONNIE:

I—I see it is.

>THE MAJOR *slips down from his chair and stands stiffly erect. The venerable* FIGURE *comes forward a little further upon the stage.* CLANCY *exclaims joyfully:*

Well now, well now—this is more like it! Welcome back to you, Sir!

MR. CONCANNON:

Thank you, thank you!

>*He turns to* THE MAJOR.

—Major Armstrong, good evening.

THE MAJOR:

How—how do you do, Sir?

MR. CONCANNON:

Much the same, thank you—much the same! And how are you, Clancy?

CLANCY:

I'm fine, Sir—just fine!

>MR. CONCANNON *seats himself and indicates the step at his feet.*

MR. CONCANNON:

Sit where I can see you.

>CLANCY *seats himself, looking up at him.* SPEEDY *re-enters quietly from the restaurant, resumes his place at the table and watches them with his hand over his*

mouth, cunning and privy. MR. CONCAN-
NON *smiles down upon* CLANCY.

What's been the trouble, my boy?

CLANCY:

Trouble?

Then, apologetically.

I'm sorry, Sir, but things in general haven't been
going quite as well as they might for me.

MR. CONCANNON:

Things in general rarely do for anyone, it seems.

CONNIE *seats herself with* THE MAJOR *at
the other table.*

CLANCY:

They've just about got me down, I'm ashamed to
admit.

MR. CONCANNON:

You?—I don't believe you, Clancy. We all of us
have our bad times, you know. Even I have had
mine.

CLANCY:

—That devil Jack Grossett—I recollect well. But
he couldn't down *you.* Why, you look younger
even than when I first saw you, though you must
have stretched sixty then.

MR. CONCANNON:

Sixty—was I ever that young?

174

CLANCY:

Anyway, it's a real treat to have a sight of you again. Where is it you've been, Sir, if I may ask?

MR. CONCANNON:

Oh—to and fro—up and down—all over, you know.

CLANCY:

That was me own itinerary, too! And when did you get back, if I may also ask?

MR. CONCANNON:

Just tonight.

CLANCY:

This very night—and didn't I do the same!

A moment, then.

And were you at the Globe by any chance, Sir?

MR. CONCANNON:

I was there.

CLANCY:

I regret deeply I had to make such a holy display of myself.

MR. CONCANNON:

You were deeply troubled: I understood that.

CLANCY:

I guess there's not much you don't understand.

MR. CONCANNON:

I have lived a long time.

CLANCY *ponders a moment before going on.*

CLANCY:

It's a fair marvel that you happened to come back just tonight. It's a matter of—of vast encouragement to me.

> *Then, carefully.*

Was there—? Did somebody—? Don't take me amiss, Sir, but was there something special that brought you?—Just precisely on this very night, you know—

> MR. CONCANNON's *smile comes and goes.*
> *Finally, with a little gesture toward*
> CLANCY, *he speaks:*

MR. CONCANNON:

It's hard to explain. Somehow, I felt impelled to come.

CLANCY:

Was it—was it as if—as if a cat jumped down on your back from a wall, maybe?

MR. CONCANNON:

Why yes—yes, that expresses it perfectly.

CLANCY:

Like me in Cleveland! Then you were—you must have been—!

> *He checks himself.*

—And how long will you be staying, if I may ask?

176

MR. CONCANNON:

That depends on you, Dan Clancy. How long do you think you will need me?

Suddenly CLANCY *bounds to his feet with a joyous shout.*

CLANCY:

Oh Glory be, it's the truth then!

MR. CONCANNON:

What, my boy?

CLANCY:

Mr. Concannon, you're the noblest, godliest man ever I've—

MR. CONCANNON:

Oh, come now!

CLANCY:

—And the fact is, that all unbeknownst to yourself, you're been sent to answer my questions for me.

CONNIE:

Dan—!

MARBLE:

Well, for the love of—!

DICKINSON:

Oh, let him get it off his chest.

CLANCY:

I regret the inconvenience, but surely it's so.

MR. CONCANNON:

Questions, you say?

177

CLANCY:

I'm near to bursting with 'em!

MR. CONCANNON:

What are they, Clancy?

CLANCY:

Well—now I'm put to it I can hardly—

He pauses.

Well, you see, I—there've been a number of things—

And pauses again.

—But I mustn't speak of myself alone. There are plenty worse off than me.

And again.

—Maybe *you* can tell me, Sir—maybe you can tell me why, for all its pretty scenery, the whole earth is full of human misery, of death and tyranny and torture? Wherever I've been, for one contented individual I've found a dozen who suffered and sweat and strained—for what?—To get their backs broken and the hope put out of their eyes.

In his excitement he rises and, still talking, paces up and down in front of the little stage.

Even the rich I've seen, leading the life of Riley, have no great look of enjoying it—on the contrary! And even the luckiest ones must die in the end.

MR. CONCANNON:

You are afraid of death?

178

CLANCY:

I don't savor the thought of it. Not while I've yet to find the meaning of life—and find it, I can't for the life of me. For from what I can make out, it's an old, old story: the ancients being as full of corruption in their time as the Sixth Ward along River Street is today.

MR. CONCANNON:

What else have you to ask?

CLANCY:

Well, Sir, to come straight out with it, if it's Good that rules over us, why is it Evil that always seems to have the upper hand?

MR. CONCANNON:

Things are not always what they seem.

CLANCY:

Begging your pardon, Sir—but that's hardly an answer. I'm well aware that misfortune sometimes makes better men of us, but just as often—in fact, oftener—we're made the worse by it. So what's a man to think?

MR. CONCANNON:

The problem of Good and Evil is a difficult one, Clancy. I expect we shall all know the answer one day.

CLANCY:

But I'd like to know now—for I'm tough, and the hereafter looks a long way away to me.

MR. CONCANNON:

After a moment.

There must be the occasions for sin, must there not—that Virtue may hold her lovely head aloft? There must be persecution, must there not—to fortify man's faith in heaven? There must be slavery, must there not—that he may know the priceless boon of freedom?

CLANCY:

Maybe there must be, but why must we *stand* 'em? Why can't we fight 'em off the face of the earth?

MR. CONCANNON:

Submission: it is the Will of God. All must be left to the Almighty Will.

CLANCY:

The same old—

CONNIE *rises and demands.*

CONNIE:

Why? Why should we be leaving everything to Him, when long ages ago He left it all to us?

CLANCY *turns and frowns at her.*

CLANCY:

How do you mean He did?

180

CONNIE:

He gave us a will of our own, didn't He? It showed too much faith in us, maybe—but give it He did. How'd you like it taken back again? A man of your build—never able so much as to think or choose for himself—how'd you like that?

CLANCY:

I wouldn't.

CONNIE:

Well, then!

> CLANCY *swings around slowly and looks at* MR. CONCANNON, *distrust and suspicion growing in his eyes.* MARBLE *speaks to* DICKINSON.

MARBLE:

It seems to me life's nothing but a sleeper-jump to death. Why can't we have more wars, and get the whole job over with?

DICKINSON:

Wars, yes! And rapes and lynchings—plagues and purges!

SPEEDY:

Life's all right. It all depends on how you live it.

> THE MAJOR *looks at him, then stumps up beside* CLANCY *and addresses* MR. CONCAN-NON *in a shaky, earnest voice.*

181

THE MAJOR:

Tell me if you will, Sir—tell me His reason for—for creating things like—like me and Ma Speedy. Why are—why are freaks?

> MR. CONCANNON *smiles, not so benevolently this time.*

MR. CONCANNON:

Would you deny Him a sense of humor?

> THE MAJOR *starts back as if struck.*

THE MAJOR:

Oh, don't—please don't—

> CLANCY *springs up angrily.*

CLANCY:

That's no thing to say! What kind of a thing is that to be saying? And every question I've asked you, you've turned off with one of your own. You're not the James Concannon *I* know! Who are you, you old devil?—

> *Suddenly he advances up the steps and upon the stage.*

Maybe the old war in Heaven came out the other way—maybe Michael the Archangel lost the fight after all—and to a crafty old rat too smart to let on that he'd won.—So we'd take *his* will as the will of God, eh?

> *He plucks the carnation from* MR. CONCANNON'S *buttonhole and flings it away.*

That would explain a lot of things, eh? Holy God, what wouldn't it!

> *Deliberately the old gentleman takes off his wig, mustache and glasses, and a familiar face smiles mockingly at* CLANCY. CLANCY *steps back.*

You—?

> SPEEDY *crows delightedly.*

SPEEDY:

The Professor! Isn't he marvelous? He had his little kit in the coat-room and did the whole change in less than— Gentlemen, the Professor!

MARBLE:

The Professor, my foot! That was an act, too. Who is it? Is it Jack Grossett himself maybe—here all along?

DICKINSON:

Why not? *He* knows this town. He knows it's the Big Time's last stand, or damn near it—and why? James Concannon! Like hell they'd come to *his* Globe, or anyone else's. They'd follow the rest to the picture houses—*he* knows!

CLANCY:

> *To* PABST.

Me life long I've thought it was Good ruled the world, but from the way you've ruled us here this night—

PABST:

How dared you interfere with a show in my theater? How dared you interrupt as smooth a bill as tonight's?

DICKINSON *rises.*

DICKINSON:

Clancy, you're right. The Devil is God now.

He draws his revolver. SPEEDY *springs up.*

SPEEDY:

Stop that! What do you think you're doing?

DICKINSON:

To PABST.

Oh you beauty, you beauty, you.—All right, Professor—relax, your act's over. It stank, Professor.

SPEEDY:

Stop it, I say!

DICKINSON:

Sit down. The guy who doubles for God has got to be good. Otherwise—

PABST *glances at* CLANCY, *smiles, and beckons to* DICKINSON.

PABST:

Come to the Globe Easter Monday.

DICKINSON:

You don't open on Monday. You're canceled—booked out!

DICKINSON *advances.*

184

MARBLE:

Easy there, boy.

DICKINSON:

I hate the evil bastard. The world'll be better for—

PABST:

Closer—come closer—

CONNIE:

No, no! Look at him—it's what he wants!

DICKINSON:

—And gets.

> *The beckoning hand is still a safe distance from the pistol. Once more* PABST *glances at* CLANCY, *then beckons again.*

PABST:

Closer—closer—a little closer—

DICKINSON:

—Sweetheart.

> *He levels the pistol. Suddenly* PABST *cries out:*

PABST:

Help me, Clancy!

CONNIE:

Watch out, Dan!

> *But* CLANCY *springs down from the stage toward* DICKINSON *just as the double discharge is heard. He buckles once, straight-*

185

> *ens again, and stands there, his eyes round*
> *with astonishment.*

CLANCY:

Well now, well now—

CONNIE:

It was another trick! Dan—are you all right?

CLANCY:

For a second I felt as if something hit me, but I feel nothing now.

> *He bears down upon* DICKINSON *and*
> *knocks the pistol from his hand.*

You!—That's no way to be doing it!

DICKINSON:

I tell you the Devil is God! Pabst is Grossett and Grossett, Concannon. And the Devil is God and we do his will!

CLANCY:

No—that's as wrong as the other! Oh, I see now it's no will of God things are as they are—no, nor Devil's will neither! It's the will of all them like himself, the world over—men bad by their own choice—and the woods full of 'em!

> *He moves toward the table, sways and*
> *braces himself against it,* CONNIE *follows*
> *him.*

CONNIE:

Dan! What is it?

186

CLANCY:

Answer? *You* gave me it!—the proud will of Man is my answer! The free will of Man, turned the wrong way. By the grace of God, free to think and choose for himself, was he?—Free to make his own world, eh? The fine job he's made of it!

> *He comes around the table laughing joylessly.*

—With pride at the top and despair at the bottom and all manner of misery in the between—turning lies into truth and truth into lies until nobody knows the one from the other—

> *He gropes for a chair and sinks into it.* CONNIE *stands over him anxiously.*

CONNIE:

Dan—what's the matter with you?

> CLANCY'S *face sets and his hand strikes the table.*

CLANCY:

But know we will, know we *will!*—For it's a fine instrument, the free will of man is, and can as easy be turned to Good as to Bad.—Ah, it's the grand thing, is man's will! Whatever it's sunk to, it can rise again. It can rise over anything, anything!

> PABST *is watching him intently.*

PABST:

Except one: Death, my poor clown.

CLANCY:

Even that! By the stars, it can live and die and resurrect itself!

PABST:

An appropriate sentiment for the day.

> CONNIE *cries out to* PABST.

CONNIE:

"Death"! What do you mean by that!

PABST:

Look at him.

> DICKINSON *and* MARBLE *move toward* CLANCY.

DICKINSON:

Clancy, for Christ's sake—

MARBLE:

You, Speedy—get some one, quick!

CONNIE:

Hurry—hurry!

CLANCY:

No! Let me be! This is me own affair.

> *But* SPEEDY *has hastened out.* CLANCY'S *head sinks.*

DICKINSON:

Clancy!

> CLANCY *turns his head and smiles sideways at him.*

188

CLANCY:

Poor John—so glorious drunk, you thought you could rid the world of evil in a blow.

PABST:

He is fantastic. He is incredible.

> *He moves toward the restaurant door.* MARBLE *moves to stop him.* PABST *gestures peremptorily.*

One side!

> CLANCY *looks up.*

CLANCY:

Let him go. There are bigger birds than him.

> MARBLE *stands aside.* PABST *addresses them all.*

PABST:

I think we may view this as an accident.—That is, unless the change at the Globe is made public. Then I am afraid we shall have to hang Dickinson.

> *He goes out.* CLANCY's *head lowers again.*

CONNIE:

Dan!

CLANCY:

Come here, girl—

> *She comes to the table, drops down into a chair beside him.*

CONNIE:

But *are* you hurt? Tell me!

189

CLANCY:

Just give me a look at you.

CONNIE:

But tell me!

CLANCY:

Do you know something?

CONNIE:

What?

CLANCY:

I like it better without.

CONNIE:

It?

CLANCY:

Your face.

CONNIE:

Without what?

CLANCY:

The little gold earrings.

CONNIE:

But what's that got to do with—?

> Then in spite of herself, she cries out
> happily:

Oh, do you, Dan?

CLANCY:

I do—and that's the truth—and me last word on the subject.

190

For a moment they gaze at each other, saying nothing. DICKINSON *begins softly:*

DICKINSON:

Once there was a little man in County Kerry and he began to pack his little bag—

> CLANCY *turns to him. There is a broad smile upon his face, and his eyes are merry.*

CLANCY:

I'll send you the postcard.

> *He makes a half gesture toward* CONNIE, *then slumps forward upon the table.*

CONNIE:

Dan!

> *He does not reply.* THE MAJOR *murmurs:*

THE MAJOR:

The things that happen. Is—is he going to die?

> CLANCY *raises his head once more.*

CLANCY:

Who is not going to?

DICKINSON:

—Those who live and die like you, Dan Clancy.

CLANCY:

Thank you, John.

> *His eyes half close. He draws a deep and satisfied breath.*

I smell the lemon tree. The air's full of it. Good-by to you all, now.

HERE COME THE CLOWNS

> *His head sinks slowly.* CONNIE *seizes his hand, clings to it desperately.*

CONNIE:

No, no! I won't let you!—Dear God, don't let him!

CLANCY:

Hush, girl. I go of me own will, where I go.

> *His head settles down upon his breast and he is still.*

CURTAIN